DO YOU KNOW . . .

- What features to look for when buying a potty chair?
- How strict to be during toilet training?
- Whether you should restrict fluids?
- The three steps to good hygiene you *must* teach?
- What to do if your child is afraid of flushing?
- How to conquer a constipation problem?
- Why older children wet the bed?
- How "sensory awareness" training may help you solve a common problem?
- What to say if your child has an "accident"?

FIND THE ANSWERS—AND MORE IN
THE TOILET TRAINING GUIDE
PARENTS CAN TRUST

TOILET TRAINING
WITHOUT TEARS

Toilet Training Without Tears

REVISED EDITION

Charles E. Shaefer, Ph.D.
with Theresa Foy DiGeronimo

Illustrations by Laura Alexander

A SIGNET BOOK

SIGNET
Published by the Penguin Group
Penguin Putnam Inc., 375 Hudson Street,
New York, New York 10014, U.S.A.
Penguin Books Ltd, 27 Wrights Lane,
London W8 5TZ, England
Penguin Books Australia Ltd, Ringwood,
Victoria, Australia
Penguin Books Canada Ltd, 10 Alcorn Avenue,
Toronto, Ontario, Canada M4V 3B2
Penguin Books (N.Z.) Ltd, 182–190 Wairau Road,
Auckland 10, New Zealand

Penguin Books Ltd, Registered Offices:
Harmondsworth, Middlesex, England

First published by Signet, an imprint of Dutton Signet,
a member of Penguin Putnam Inc.

First Printing, Revised Edition, November, 1997
First Printing, November, 1989

10 9 8 7 6 5 4 3

PUBLISHER'S NOTE
The ideas, procedures, and suggestions contained in this book are not intended as a substitute for consulting with your physician. All matters regard-
ing your health require medical supervision.

To our children
Eric and Karine
and
Matt, Joey, and Colleen,
who gave us many years of practical experience

CONTENTS

ACKNOWLEDGMENTS

We would like to thank our agent, Faith Hamlin, for her continued support and encouragement. Also, we give a thankful nod to our former editor, Alexia Dorszynski, who knew from the start that this book would be around for a long time.

We owe a debt of gratitude to all the neighborhood moms who shared their tales of the toilet with good humor and candor.

A Few Words Before

Learning to use the toilet is a milestone in your child's development. Like learning to walk or talk, it is something that takes patience and time, as well as a particular degree of physical and intellectual ability. But learning to use the toilet is different from many of the other things your child learns because it is often a source of great concern and distress for both you and your child.

There is often good reason for this concern. A stressful toilet-training period can damage an otherwise good parent/child relationship. It can lower a child's sense of self-esteem. And because some parents become angry when their children learn slowly or make mistakes, toilet training is not uncommonly the cause of physical/psychological abuse.

On the other hand, when toilet training goes well, it fosters a child's sense of independence and accomplishment. It strengthens the bonds of a good parent/child relationship. And it gives both parent and child a feeling of satisfaction. What better reasons can there be for learning how to toilet train without bringing your child to the point of tears?

There are several methods that can be used to give your child a positive toilet-training experience, and this book will help you choose the one that is best for you and your child. It will also help you deal with the conflicts and problems you may already be experiencing if your child is three-and-a-half years old or older and not yet toilet-trained.

Most children eventually learn how to use the toilet. The approaches to toilet training explained in this book, however, have an advantage over many other methods because each of them teaches this natural skill in a positive, nurturing way—without yelling, threatening, punishing, ridiculing, or spanking, and so, without tears. For many parents these approaches may be very different from those they are familiar with.

As you read through this book, you'll notice that all children are referred to as "he." This is not to imply in any way that only boys need positive toilet-training strategies—as any parents of a little girl who is learning to use the potty can tell you. It is done in the name of simplicity and uniformity since the alternative of talking about a "he or she" kind of person seems a bit confusing and impersonal. All the information is applicable to all boys AND girls who are trying to learn the skills involved in mature toileting habits, and for their parents who want to teach them with warmth and encouragement.

When you venture into the realm of toilet training, I'd be delighted to hear about your successes as well as your frustrations. Your feedback is the kind of information that will help me to help other parents in the future.

Send your letters to:

Dr. Charles Schaefer
139 Temple Avenue
Hackensack, New Jersey 07601

PART I

Basic Toilet Training

Chapter One

An Adventure in Parenting

Take a deep breath, sit back, and relax. You're about to take your child on a trip through the realm of toilet training. It's a trip that can be exciting for both of you, and it will lead your child out of diapers and set the stage for his growing sense of independence. It's also a trip that will provide you with an opportunity to strengthen the bonds of your parent/child relationship.

If this optimistic view of toilet training sounds like it's too good to be true, then take a minute to rethink your feelings. Some parents dread toilet training because they've heard horror stories about temper tantrums, clashes of wills, messy accidents, and shouting matches. But you're not embarking on a frightening mystery ride—it's a natural and inevitable rite of passage for you and your child. With the knowledge you'll gain from this book, you'll know exactly where you're going every step of the way, and your child can have a toilet-training experience that is truly without tears.

As with any other trip, you'll be better able to enjoy the adventure and avoid major problems if you plan ahead. I've written this book to help you do just that. You'll learn the facts, find the supplies you'll need, be able to make provisions for the comfort of your child, know in advance how to handle possible trouble spots and, most important, you'll be mapping out a course that will be best for *you* and *your child*.

Although just the thought of toilet training makes

some parents and children feel uncertain and anxious, you'll soon discover that this process needn't be an awful ordeal. The more knowledge and guidance you have, however, the smoother and happier the training period will be. The wealth of research information now available on a variety of toilet-training methods gives you an advantage over the parents of past generations. You can choose the one that best fits your needs and the needs of your child.

The drawback in having so much information, however, is that you must gather it all together and then sort it out. Your parents may suggest one approach; your grandparents swear by another. Your best friend whispers about the psychological damage that improper training may do to a child, while your neighbor rattles off facts about the physical development of the central nervous system and its relationship to toilet training. Child-rearing books and magazine articles send you in wildly different directions. It's nice to have many options, but it can also be confusing.

My goal in writing this book has been to gather together all the available information, to sort out the research, the scientific studies, and the most effective methods of toilet training, and then present them in a way that will make it simple for you to understand. First I'll present some basic principles of toilet training; then I'll explain four possible methods. In Part II, I'll give detailed programs for training children who have not mastered bladder and/or bowel control by the age of three and a half. In Part III, I will discuss toilet training with a caregiver and while traveling. And finally, in Part IV, I will give guidelines for training mentally and physically challenged children. Each parent and child pair has individual needs; there is no one right or wrong method of toilet training. In this book, each method stands on its own. After you read through each of them, you can decide for yourself when it will be best to train your child and how you want to do it.

Parents have not always had this freedom of choice. In the last century, the toilet-training methods recommended most often reflected the popular developmental theories of the day, theories that often were used to measure the quality of one's parenting skills. In the

1920s and 1930s, for example, behavioral psychologists believed that behavioral development resulted from conditioning; the sooner the conditioning began, they reasoned, the sooner a child would master a desired pattern of behavior. This belief led to an approach of early and strict toilet training that emphasized great control, close monitoring, and rigid scheduling. A 1935 publication by the U.S. Children's Bureau suggests that toilet training could begin shortly after birth. If not, it continued, "it should always be begun by the third month and be completed by the eighth month." Parents also received instructions for "using the soap stick as an aid in conditioning the rectum."[1]

In the 1940s and 1950s more permissive attitudes developed in response to two new developmental theories. Some psychoanalytical psychologists asserted that toilet training could be the root of later tensions and conflicts that would affect one's personality for a lifetime. Developmental psychologists, on the other hand, believed that the ability to control one's toilet habits depended on a child's physiological development and maturation. Both groups advocated delaying training until the child was at least eight months old, and a 1957 study found that 50 percent of parents began toilet training on or before nine months.[2]

In the 1960s a theory of gradualism took the 1950s approach one step further. Toilet training became a child-oriented process in which parents and children gradually tried out portions of mature toileting behaviors when the child was physically and psychologically ready. Typically, American children in 1967 had control of their bowels sometime between eighteen and twenty-four months and had day and nightime bladder control by age four and a half. It is probably no coincidence that this gradual approach to training became popular at the same time that most American households had their own washing machines, and when disposable diapers made their debut.

In 1973 psychologists Foxx and Azrin introduced a rapid method of toilet training that is, like the methods of the 1920s and 1930s, based on the theory of behavioral conditioning.[3] With this method, children as young as 20 months old can complete the toilet-training process in as little as 24 hours. It's no wonder that this approach became popular in an age when the two-career family had become the norm, with time for toilet training short and out-of-home child care common.

In the past, the "right" age to begin training also depended on where you lived—the methods varied by geographic locale as well as by era. A 1965 study found that the age of training varies from one culture to another. In London, for example, the average training began at 4.6 months; in Paris at 7.8 months; in Stockholm at 12.4 months.[4] Anthropologists have found evidence of a variety of toilet training methods even among primitive tribes. Although some tribes use an approach that is unstructured and lenient, others, like the East African Digo tribe, follow an early and regimented method. According to a 1977 study, parents in this tribe begin toilet training with a calm, nurturing, conditioning approach soon after birth and usually achieve day and night dryness by five or six months.[5] This same kind of gentle, caring approach is also often used in China to achieve full control of bladder and bowel by eighteen months of age.[6]

The historical and cultural studies of toilet training methods make it apparent that it is not the age of the child that is most influential in toilet training. Regardless of when training begins, it is the parent's attitude, the gentleness or severity of approach, and the state of preparedness that dictate the ease or difficulty of the process.

To prepare for toilet training without tears, it's important that you don't jump right into one of the approaches outlined in this book without reading Chapter Two first. The information in this chapter will help you get ready. I will explain the physical and psychological developmental stages of your child's growth so that you will understand his abilities and needs. I'll teach you how to take on the positive attitude that will reduce stress and cool tempers if the going starts to get rough, and I'll share some toilet training stories and concerns that other parents have told me over the years.

The information in Chapter Two will also help you get set. I'll make suggestions about the types and the use of potty seats and deal with the problems of training a child while you're at work outside the home. I'll talk about the vocabulary to use with your child, and I'll give you a general list of do's and don'ts. All of this information will help you toilet train your child without tears, no matter which method you choose.

The toilet-training approaches I've included in this book are presented in the order I've outlined below; I'm not recommending one over another. Although some methods are faster than others, and some may be easier than others, all are effective methods.

1. The Readiness Approach (page 54) is the most popular method at this time. Training begins when the child shows clear signs of physical, intellectual, and psychological readiness. This usually happens when children are between eighteen months to two and a half years of age. When the child is fully ready, training can usually be accomplished in a few months.

2. The Early Training Approach (page 81) is a method for toilet training infants from age three months to one year. It requires a great deal of parental persistence and patience, and it usually takes many months to complete training.

3. The Rapid Approach (page 102) is a method that can be used to train children twenty months of age and older in a 24-hour period.

4. The Intensive Approaches for children delayed in learning to use the toilet (pages 113-183) are appropriate methods for children who are not toilet trained by age three and a half. These approaches combine several techniques to provide increased leverage on the developmentally delayed child.

Toilet training is actually a form of time travel. Your destination is a time when your child has mature toileting habits. The route you take depends largely on your good judgement and personal preference. So take another deep breath, look ahead with optimism, and use this book as your guide to finding an approach and gathering the information that will make it easy for you to toilet train your child without tears.

Chapter Two

Ready, Set, Go

Before you begin toilet training, you must prepare yourself and your child. This chapter will help you to do that in three stages. It will explain what to do as you get ready; it will detail how you can get set, and then with these basics in hand, you'll be ready to go through the rest of this book to select the method of toilet training you want to use.

Get Ready

A Positive Attitude

Regardless of the method of toilet training you choose to use, or the age you decide to begin, your attitude toward the training process and toward your child will influence your ability to achieve toilet training without tears. Since attitude is such an important factor in toilet training, it's the first thing you should examine and prepare in this "get ready" stage.

At the university clinic where I teach, I often conduct toilet-training classes for parents. At our first meeting, I ask the parents to take turns talking about their attitudes toward toilet training. This helps them examine their feelings; then after some discussion they can decide if they need to readjust the way they view the toilet-training process.

20

Elaine and Ted spoke out at a recent gathering. "This is something we feel Roy should do now, and so he will do it," said Ted. "It's as simple as that because if he doesn't, he'll be punished." As they continued to speak, it became apparent that Elaine and Ted had set high expectations for Roy; up to that point he had always been able to meet them. They demanded obedience and so he was obedient. Their expectation was that because toilet training was a high priority right now, they would tell Roy what they wanted him to do; then they would persistently follow a strict routine of training, and then Roy would be toilet trained. "This isn't a time to be wishy-washy," said Elaine. "A child needs to be told what's expected of him and that nothing less is acceptable."

Elaine and Ted have an attitude about toilet training that is intense, strict, and demanding. As they spoke, many of the other parents nodded their heads in agreement. One of my goals in working with these parents and in writing this book for you is to dispel this kind of attitude. Although cold and severe training regimes have been used over the years to "successfully" toilet train many children, these children certainly were not trained without trauma or tears.

Judy and Fred, on the other hand, said that they did not feel that toilet training should be categorized as a discipline matter. "Most children want to please their parents," said Fred. "I know our Debbie will try to use the potty when we ask her, but we're not going to make a big deal of it. If she really doesn't like it, or if she has a lot of accidents, we'll love her anyway, clean up the mess, and try again another time." Judy said she knew that some people (like her mother) would tell them that they should be sterner in their approach, but she and Fred felt uncomfortable about scolding or punishing Debbie for things over which they weren't sure she had real control.

Judy and Fred had stumbled onto the kind of patient and tolerant attitude that is the core of toilet training without tears. As you get ready to toilet train your child, make a real effort to set your attitude on par with Judy and Fred. At first it will be easy to say, "Sure, I'll be matter of fact, understanding, tolerant, and warm," but when the training sessions begin, you may find that it will take more than just good intentions to maintain this positive attitude. It will take a thorough understanding of exactly what "positive attitude" means. We often throw around abstract words like "warm," "patient," and "tolerant," without really thinking about what we're saying. Think about the following attitude descriptions as you get ready to toilet train your child:

- Matter-of-fact: To have a matter-of-fact attitude, you must be straightforward and unemotional. This attitude will give your child the message that the elimination process is a normal and natural one, a fact of daily living—not something supernaturally wonderful, not horrendously awful.
- Tolerant: If you adopt a tolerant attitude, you will be able to endure events that are not in line with what you had hoped or planned for. When your child sits on the potty for 10 minutes with no results, for example, then soils his diaper 30 seconds after you put it back on, you'll be able to stay calm and accepting.
- Understanding: To be understanding during toilet training, you need to create a sympathetic yet friendly relationship with your child. You can cultivate your ability to be understanding by learning about your child's state of physical and emotional development. The information on pages 24-31 will help you. With an understanding attitude you'll be able to comprehend your child's frustration and failures, his triumphs and successes.
- Warm: During the toilet-training period, show your child unfaltering love and affection. Make a point of offering lots of hugs and smiles. Let your child know that if an accident happens, your arms will always be a safe place to run to.

Your Role

Along with developing a positive attitude, you'll also need to determine exactly what role you play in the toilet-training process. Ask yourself these questions:

- What's my job during this training period?
- How much influence on the outcome do I really have?
- How much pressure should I apply?

You can start to find the answers to these questions by looking at two extreme views that many parents wrongly believe define their role in the toilet-training process.

Some parents take a permissive role during toilet training because they believe that toilet "training" is an intrusive approach to a natural process. They believe that if left alone, all children will eventually teach themselves how to use the toilet. Therefore, these parents leave the learning of bowel and bladder control almost entirely up to the child. Although it's true that learning to control the bowel and bladder is a developmental process (see page 24 for a detailed explanation), all children can benefit from some guidance as they develop this skill. Some studies have found a connection between the permissive approach and the continuous type of encopretic child (a child who has never developed bowel control for any sustained period of time). Most experts now believe that children learn best with some parental help in attaining mature toileting.

On the other hand, some parents take a very severe, punitive role during toilet training. A number still believe that a child must be toilet trained in much the same way a puppy is paper trained, with a "rub-his-nose-in-it" approach. They rely on repeated scolding, spanking, yelling, and harsh punishment. Studies have found, however, that a severe approach does nothing to stop children from wetting or soiling their pants, nor does it reduce the time needed for toilet training. In fact, there is abundant evidence that very severe toilet training can cause such harmful consequences as negativism, aggressiveness, fearfulness, compulsiveness, rigid behavior, rage, guilt, excessive cleanliness, and defiance. Judy and Fred are right; toilet training is not a discipline problem. There is no room for a drill sergeant in the bathroom.

What exactly does "permissive" and "very severe" mean? The following material is from a study by Sears, Maccoby, and Levin.[1] It defines the roles parents can play during toilet training, from the permissive "not at

all severe" role, to the punitive "very severe" role. Read
through these definitions. Your job will then be to find
a middle ground with which you'll be comfortable training your child.

DEGREES OF PARENTAL PRESSURE

1. *Not at all severe:* The child more or less trains himself. It is not his fault when he has accidents; they
   are considered natural. There is no punishment or
   scolding.
2. *Slight pressure:* There is mild disapproval for some
   late accidents. Parents make efforts to show child
   where, when, and how to go to the toilet.
3. *Moderate pressure:* Child receives scoldings for
   some late deviations; parents set up a routine of
   fairly frequent toileting.
4. *Fairly severe training:* The child is scolded fairly
   often, parent clearly shows disapproval. The child
   may be left on the toilet for fairly lengthy periods.
5. *Very severe training:* The child is punished severely
   for deviations; parents are angry and emotional
   over them.

Consider your role in the toilet-training process to be
that of a teacher—a teacher who is neither too strict nor
too lenient. The information in the rest of this chapter
will help you find the middle ground and will aid you in
developing that all-important positive attitude.

The Basic Principles of Development

Before you ask your child to gain complete voluntary
control over the elimination process, take time to consider exactly what that involves. Sometimes a child is
not physically able to be completely trained because his
neuromuscular system is not yet mature enough to perform the way you want it to. Toilet training without tears
may be impossible if this aspect of training is
overlooked.

The openings of the rectum (where bowel movements

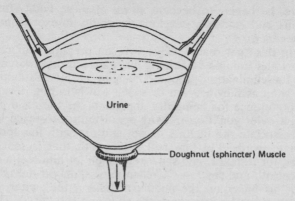

The bladder

exit) and of the bladder (where urine is stored) are usually kept closed by circular sphincter muscles. (The root
"sphin" comes from a Greek word meaning "to shut
tight.") In adults, the sphincter muscles are called voluntary muscles because an adult can purposely tighten the
muscle to hold back the urine or bowel movement; when
enough urine or excrement is stored in the bladder or
rectum, an adult can relax the sphincter muscles to release the contents.

These voluntary muscles of the excretory system work
in conjunction with the involuntary actions of the digestive system to process our food and prepare it for elimination. Involuntary functions begin in the esophagus,
which brings our food to the stomach; then the food
is passed on to the small intestine, where nutrients are
absorbed for use in the body. The remainder of the food
is emptied into the large intestine, where water is absorbed from it, and the remaining waste is stored for
elimination.

Unlike an adult, a newborn's entire process of diges-
tion and elimination is involuntary; it is controlled by
the gastrocolonic reflex. A newborn does not feel the
sensation of a full bladder or bowel and has no control
over where or when his urine and BMs will be released.
As an infant takes in food, his entire intestinal tract is
activated and the sphincter muscles relax involuntarily.
As the child's central nervous and muscular systems ma-

ture, he begins to become aware of these bodily functions, and gradually develops the ability to exert control over them.

In this "get ready" stage you can prepare your child for toilet training by helping him gain sensory awareness of the elimination process. Changing an infant's diapers as soon as they are wet or soiled will help him develop a preference for being dry and clean. As the child gets a bit older you'll have many opportunities to teach him to associate the feelings of wet and dry with the appropriate words. Let him feel a facecloth that is soaking wet, for instance, and say "wet"; then let him feel a dry facecloth and say "dry." When juice spills on the table, put his finger on the puddle and say "wet"; after you clean it up, let him touch the spot and say "dry." Then you can begin to help him realize when he's urinating or defecating by watching for the signs like grimacing, grunting, a reddening face, or a sudden stillness. Say, "You're making BMs in your diaper," or, "Do you feel your diaper getting warm and wet? That's caused by your urine." Toilet training at any age and with any method will be easier if the child understands that urine and BMs come out of his body and he has some control over when that happens.

Although many child development experts assert that toilet training will be successful only when a child has complete voluntary control over the elimination process, there is debate over the age at which this can occur. One popular study says that voluntary bowel and urinary control will occur at about one and a half to two years of age.[2] Another study holds that complete control of sphincter muscles will be attained between fifteen and eighteen months.[3] Yet another says that consistent voluntary control of the sphincter muscles is not possible before the age of two.[4] Although this debate on readiness continues, it is also true that many children throughout history and in many different cultures have been successfully toilet trained before they are one year of age. This fact makes it apparent that even the very young child has some ability to control the sphincter muscles.

At this point, it is clear that we still do not fully understand exactly the chain of events involved in the elimination process. We don't know exactly when there is full control of the voluntary sphincter muscles, what the specific relationship between the involuntary and voluntary muscles is, nor how the use of these muscles is affected by the environment (the particular method used and/or the parental attitudes). Given this uncertainty, it's easy to see why methods of toilet training have broken into several schools of thought. Some say a child cannot be toilet trained before twelve months of age. Others say it's too late to start training after the age of fifteen months because once the child has learned to use the word "no," the stage is set for a long, drawn-out battle. Some say it is best to wait until a child wants to be trained, which may not happen until three or four years of age. Some say toilet training is a slow, gradual process; others say it can be done in one day.

You can successfully toilet train your child with a method based on any one of these theories as long as you remember this important fact: Your child is unique, unlike all other children. His individual needs, abilities, physical development, and level of emotional maturity all play a part in determining which method of toilet training will work best for him. No one knows your child better than you; thus no one can tell you when or how you must toilet train him.

Although it is impossible to prescribe the best age and the best method of toilet training for your child, some aspects of toilet training can be applied to most children. The sequence of bowel and bladder control, for example, is usually obtained in this order:

1. Child gains control of bowels while asleep
2. Child gains control of bowels while awake
3. Child gains control of bladder while awake
4. Child gains control of bladder while asleep

There are several reasons why most children will attain bowel control before bladder control:

- The bowel requires less complicated muscle coordination.

- It is easier for the sphincter muscle to hold onto a solid substance than a liquid one, as you quickly learn when you have diarrhea.
- The urge to defecate occurs fewer times in the course of a day than the urge to urinate. There is, then, less chance for bowel-control accidents.
- Children don't feel as possessive of urine as they do of BMs. This possessiveness generates greater awareness and care of its elimination.

Some children can complete this entire bowel/bladder control sequence very quickly—somewhere between one day and one week. Others may take several years to gain complete control during both day and night hours. But generally, when signs of voluntary control are evident, most children complete the training in less than six months.

The information on facing page 30, adapted from a study by Ilg and Ames,[5] will give you some idea of the timetable many children follow as they mature physically and emotionally.

Although the sequence of bowel and bladder daytime/nighttime control is generally the same for all children, the age at which they can complete the sequence is actually quite varied. The box lists *average* developmental progressions. Some children progress slower, others faster. There are, however, other time factors that remain fairly constant. For example, girls often train earlier and faster than boys, and children who are advanced in their large motor development skills, such as sitting, crawling, and walking, may train sooner than other children.

It's also true that although research has found that very young children—under one year of age—can be toilet trained, the total time required to complete their toilet training is usually longer than it is for children who start at a relatively later age. One study found that children who begin training before five months take an average of 10 months to complete the training successfully. Children who begin when they are twenty months or more take an average of five months to complete the training successfully. This study also found that the children who show the fewest emotional problems during training are those who begin between five and fourteen months, or who begin after nineteen months. This is often the case because a child who is between fourteen and nineteen months is just beginning to exert his growing sense of independence. As he learns to use the word "no," any attempt at toilet training may turn into a battle of wills. He is also becoming more mobile and thereafter anything that makes him sit still for a prolonged period might be met with rebellion and resistance. Many parents find it easier to begin toilet training before this phase begins, or to delay it until the "automatic no" phase starts to subside, usually around twenty to twenty-four months.

No matter what age you begin toilet training, you can expect occasional regressions; they are a natural part of growth and learning. In many other areas of learning, your child will grasp a concept and then forget it, then try it again and forget some of it, until finally one day he masters all of it. Don't let your child's "three steps forward, one step back" routine upset you—it's bound to happen. Many parents tell the same kind of story: "My child went five straight days without a single accident. So I put him in regular underwear when we went to visit my inlaws. As soon as we got there, he wet all over their couch."

Although regression to wet and soiled pants happens as a natural part of development, it can also happen at times that are somewhat predictable. For example, if your child is at a point of rapid advancement in some other area of development, such as learning to walk, talk, or climb, he may become so involved with that new skill that he'll forget what he's learned about bladder and/or bowel control. Or, if your child feels emotionally stressed, nervous, tense, or under pressure, due to illness, new surroundings, or a new baby, he may be unable to concentrate on the sensory cues that signal the need to pass BMs and urine. Expect regression so that you won't lose your resolve to play the role of a warm and tolerant teacher when it happens.

The more you know about the individual nature of your child's physical and emotional state, the better you'll be able to understand the problems that may occur during toilet training. The fact that some babies

4 weeks: An infant may cry during sleep when wetting and there may be a moment of wakefulness.

16 weeks: The number of daily bowel movements decreases as the volume of each one increases.

1 year: A child may attain dryness after a nap. He may show intolerance of wetness at certain times of the day. One in 100 children will stay dry through the night with or without toilet training experience.

15 months: Some children like to sit on the toilet and may pass urine or BMs; at other times they resist. Their ability to retain urine and BMs has lengthened to a span of 2 or 3 hours. However, placing a child on the toilet may cause him to withhold urine, and he may then release the urine as soon as he is removed from the toilet.

1–2 years: Children attain nighttime bowel control

18 months: A child can respond with nod or shake of the head when asked if he wants to use the potty; this shows that he can now relate the words to the function. He may report accidents by pulling at his pants. Voluntary control may begin.

21 months: A child reports accidents by pointing at his puddles. He usually tells you after wetting, but sometimes before. He is pleased with his successes, but the number of daily urinations may start to increase and so the accidents may multiply.

2 years: The child has better control. He shows no resistance to routines. He verbalizes his toilet needs fairly consistently. He may go into the bathroom and pull down his own pants. Bowel control may become established as child attains voluntary control of the sphincter muscle.

2½ years: The child is able to hold urine in bladder for as long as 5 hours. Two-thirds of children will be dry most of the time. Most are partially trained for daytime bladder control, and nighttime wetting may start to come under control.

3 years: The child has few bowel or bladder accidents. He may be dry all night.

4 years: Almost all children have complete daytime/nighttime bowel and bladder control.

can begin training at five months doesn't mean all children can or should. The fact that the little girl next door hasn't accidentally soiled her pants since she was twelve months old doesn't mean that your thirteen-month-old is deliberately defying you when he soils his pants. Although some children can walk at ten months, not all are physically able to do so. Most parents realize that scolding and punishing a ten-month-old who can't yet walk across the room like her cousin will not make her walk any sooner than she is able to. Like walking, the physical ability to toilet train is best fostered with patience, encouragement, and practice.

There is a complex relationship between the principles of physical development and a child's ability to gain mastery over the elimination process. What is most important for you to remember is that the development of the neuromuscular system plays a role in your child's toilet-training experience and that all children develop at different rates. If you understand the developmental process, you may even be able to stay calm when exactly 30 seconds after your fifteen-month-old emphatically says he doesn't have to have a BM, everyone in the room can smell that, in fact, he did need to go to the potty.

Know Yourself

As you get ready to toilet train your child, some aspects about yourself and the way you view the toilet-training process need to be examined. Knowing yourself can be just as important as knowing your child when you want to have a positive and tearless training experience.

Emotional Control

The ideal attitude for toilet training without tears is one that is tolerant and understanding. As I explained in the last section, knowing the relationship between physical maturity and toileting control should help you adopt this attitude. But even when you understand the role of physiology, maintaining a tolerant attitude is sometimes easier said than done. We'll discuss common toilet-training problems and setbacks later in this book, with attention to the problems that may occur with each method of training. Before you even choose a method, however, you can cultivate a mental attitude that will help you handle frustrating situations and maintain your sense of understanding.

"I know I'm doing all the wrong things," confessed one young mother. "I know I shouldn't yell at my daughter when she doesn't tell me she has to go to the potty. But sometimes, especially when things are hectic around the house, I just can't help myself." Most parents will agree that it's frustrating to work long and hard at toilet training and then wake up one morning with a child who acts like he's never heard the word "potty" before. But however frustrated you may become, always remember that you're in control of the emotional tone of this toilet-training experience. Most children react to situations in the same way that their parents react. If the parent becomes upset and angry, so will the child. If the parent says, "This child will never be toilet trained," the child is likely to believe it. If, on the other hand, the parent remains calm when faced with a problem, so will the child. If the parent is always positive and confident and says, "You'll do better next time," or "I know you'll be able to use the toilet very soon," the child will also be positive and confident.

If you find yourself ready to react with anger to a toilet-training problem—stop. Count to ten. Then tell yourself that you will not begin a fight that will discourage and frighten your child. There is not one piece of evidence to support the belief that if you yell loud enough or hit hard enough, a child will stop soiling and/or wetting. Harsh scolding or beating a child won't solve the problem; it will only further aggravate a tense situation.

You can also prepare yourself to maintain a tolerant attitude by imagining beforehand what you will say when your child doesn't perform the way you want him to. You should avoid saying things like:

- "You're such a baby!"
- "You're not very smart, are you?"
- "If you loved me, you'd go to the potty."

Verbal abuse is just as destructive as physical abuse. A child needs a sense of confidence and self-esteem to master new developmental tasks. Every time a parent ridicules, demeans, or hurts a child with cruel or thoughtless words during toilet training, they both take several steps backward. The "Get Set" section in this chapter will explain the best way to talk to your child about toilet training.

Personal Feelings About Bodily Functions and Cleanliness

Acknowledging your personal feelings about the elimination process, as well as the body parts involved in this function, is another way to strengthen your ability to be positive and supportive during toilet training.

When you change your child's soiled diapers, do you do so with obvious disgust? Do you attend to his needs while scrunching up your nose and muttering, "Pee-yew, you stink!" Does a full diaper load make you gag? If you've done these things in the past, you may have already given your child the message that urinating and defecating are dirty and revolting activities. The toilet-training process will run much smoother if you can accept the elimination of bodily wastes as the natural, physical function that it is.

Children need to know that everyone urinates and has BMs, and that it is normal and acceptable behavior. They should never feel embarrassed by this process. Sometimes we have more tolerance and respect for strangers who pass gas on the bus than we do for our own children who have no defense against embarrassing tongue-lashings like: "Did you dirty your pants again? You should be ashamed of yourself. All these people don't want to smell you. I thought you were a big boy, but I guess you're just a baby . . ." and on . . . and on. . . .

Without realizing it, sometimes parents teach their children to associate the act of urinating and defecating with being dirty and shameful. They learn this through the kind of direct dialogue described earlier, and they learn it through the indirect route of body language— the scrunched-up nose, the scowls, and the frowns. Why should a child make an effort to bring forth something that his parents ridicule or loathe? Sometimes, children who are afraid of being "dirty" may become constipated in their effort to hold back. Plan to make a real effort during toilet training to emphasize the natural and necessary aspect of elimination.

There are certainly times when it is difficult to be casual about a toilet mess. It is not uncommon, for example, for children to play with their BMs—to squish them through their toes, to paint with them on the walls, to clap them through their fingers, to smear them into the rug, or even to eat them. Little boys sometimes entertain themselves by urinating on the walls, on the floor, or even into their own faces—or yours if you're not careful. Of course this isn't behavior to be praised or a situation to be ignored, but it is important to remember if this happens that your child is being naturally curious and playful. Expressing your disgust and revulsion will give your child the wrong message about his bodily functions. Instead, use this opportunity to remind your child that everyone—Grandma, Grandpa, Mom and Dad, sister, brother, and friends—makes BMs and urinates, but they put them in the toilet because that's the way to stay nice and clean. Explain that it is not acceptable to play with urine or BMs or to put them anyplace except the toilet or potty. Then lead your child to water, finger paints, clay, or other acceptable alternatives that will satisfy his curiosity and need for the pleasure of physical manipulation.

Another danger in associating the elimination process with dirty, shameful acts is the chance that the child may generalize the "dirty" quality of elimination to his or her sexual body parts. Some studies have found a relationship between sexual problems and a very strict, prudish, toilet-training experience. The penis, the vagina, and the anus are all body parts that perform necessary functions just like the mouth, fingers, and toes. As you get ready to toilet train your child, take time to neutralize your own feelings about bodily functions and body parts, about urine and excrement, and about modesty and sexuality.

Motives for Training

Why do you want to toilet train your child now? Of course, like most parents, you want to teach him to be clean and independent, and you want to guide him along as he gains mastery over his bodily functions. However, you won't be able to do this in a supportive and positive way, if you begin to toilet train because your brother's daughter was trained at this age and you'll feel incompetent if your son takes longer. Or perhaps you're doing it because your mother says you should—all five of *her* children were completely trained before their first birthday. Maybe you're doing it because all the other children of the same age in your neighborhood are already in training pants. Perhaps your pediatrician suggested this age and now you feel like you're in competition for some kind of blue ribbon award. Or is it possible that you strive for perfection in all things and your child's soiled and wet diapers are upsetting your view of order in the world? Maybe you're just tired of changing diapers and want your child to do things your way for once. If you're toilet training your child for any of these reasons, you're certainly not alone. Family pressure, social expectations, and personal needs are common reasons for trying to toilet train children. Unfortunately, these motives rarely lead to a toilet-training experience that is without tears.

The success of each approach described in this book relies on a commonsense attitude: "I want to toilet train my child at this age and with this method because I think he's capable of doing it; so I want to give it a try." Don't let anyone else push you and your child into something that neither of you wants to do at this time.

The Right Time

As you get ready for toilet training, take a good look at your family calendar. Plan the training period at a time when you will be most consistently available to work with your child, and a time that is relatively free from outside obligations. It will be easier to maintain a positive and calm attitude toward toilet training if you and your child are not trying to deal with other stressful situations at the same time.

If you are a working parent, it might be best to begin toilet training when you have time off from work. This will give you a 'round-the-clock opportunity to use whichever method you decide on to its fullest advantage.

If that's not possible, then choose a time when you probably won't be called out of town, or when you can avoid working overtime. If at all practical, it's also helpful if you can toilet train during warm-weather months. It is easier to stay calm when a child wets or soils while outside than when he's sitting on your bed. It's also easier to make the necessary trips to the bathroom if you don't have to deal with boots and snowsuits. Outdoor training is also an excellent way to teach sensory awareness. Let your child run around naked or wearing only underwear. When he urinates and defecates, he will immediately feel and see the result. Diapers, especially the newer, thinner, more absorbent, disposable kind, make it difficult for a child to realize what the process of elimination is all about. The warm weather gives you an ideal and natural way to teach him.

In addition to arranging the training period around your work schedule and warm weather, avoid toilet training your child at the following times:

- During a holiday season. You will be too rushed and busy to give your child the attention he needs, and your child will be too wound up to answer when nature calls.
- Immediately after a death or while there is grave illness in the family. Your nerves will be in no shape to handle the stress of teaching a new skill at that time, and your child will know that something is wrong or different. This may make him less cooperative than usual.
- When there is something new in your child's life. A new school, a new home, a new baby-sitter, or a new baby will drain your child's store of energy and weaken his powers of concentration. It will usually be more difficult and take longer to train under these kinds of circumstances. New ventures will also sap your ability to give your full attention to the process of toilet training.

Learning mature toileting habits is a normal developmental task that almost all people eventually master. To learn this process without stress or tears, your child needs your unconditional love, your guidance, support, and encouragement. But sometimes the going can get rough. If you're ever tempted to throw up your hands in despair, or to do something that will make your child cry, reread this chapter. Occasionally you may need to renew your intent to have a tolerant and supportive attitude, to redefine your role in the toilet-training process, to remind yourself about the basic developmental principles involved in toileting. It will also be helpful to reexamine your personal feelings about bodily functions and cleanliness, recheck your motives for training, and reevaluate the time period you've chosen to begin toilet training.

Get Set

By this time you understand the importance of a positive attitude, you know the kind of role you should play in the training process, you understand the developmental factors that influence toilet training, and you're aware of the personal factors that affect a child's ability to toilet train without tears. Now it's time to "get set" for toilet training by getting the right equipment, by establishing an appropriate vocabulary to use with your child, by engaging the support of all people who will be involved with your child during the toilet-training period, and by making your spouse an equal partner in this toilet-training venture.

Equipment

Potty chair

Many parents find that toilet training is easier and that their children are more cooperative if they have a potty chair. This is probably because a potty chair feels safer and is more comfortable than a full-size toilet. A good potty chair has a high back and side arms for support. It has a secure broad base, with rubber tips to prevent sliding, and ideally, it has a wooden seat that does not feel as cold as those made of plastic.

Children also like to have something of their very own that's like Mommy's and Daddy's. Potty chairs are personal possessions that children are usually very proud of. These chairs can help your child imitate you and at the same time teach him to be less dependent on you. Since your child should be able to get on and off by himself, don't buy the type of chair that has any kind of animal or cartoon head sticking up in front. You should also make sure the deflector cup (the shield that is used to keep a little boy's urine from spraying around the room) is detachable so you'll be able to throw it away. A boy (or girl for that matter) could easily hurt himself getting on or off a seat when the deflector cup is attached. Rather than use the cup, it's better to simply teach your son to aim his penis downward while he's sitting. Most little boys learn bladder control while sitting on the potty because it's best not to confuse them with stand-up/sit-down training. Once they feel comfortable about contracting and relaxing the sphincter muscle (at about two years old) they can more easily be taught to urinate while standing up.

Eventually, your child should also be responsible for helping to dump the urine or BMs from the potty chair into the toilet. Therefore, the chair's bowl should be easy to detach without being so loose that it will slip, jolt, or wiggle when your child sits down. (The potty chair bowl will be easier to clean if you leave an inch of water in the bottom at all times.)

A potty chair is also desirable during training because it allows the child to sit securely with his feet on the floor. This is important because it gives him the leverage he needs to contract the lower abdominal muscles and push out BMs. Without this leverage a child could strain the muscles around the anus as he tries to bear down.

A potty chair can be especially useful during training because it reduces many of the toilet anxieties that children sometimes have. Some children are afraid of the height of the adult toilet; others are afraid of falling through the adult seat into the bowl, and some are afraid of the noise that flushing makes. Because a potty chair is close to the ground, has a child-size seat, and does not flush, it lessens some of the anxiety your child may feel about learning bowel and bladder control.

Useful as potty chairs are, they do have a few drawbacks you should be aware of. If a child is trained on a potty chair, for instance, he may not be willing to use an adult-size toilet when you're out of the house shopping, visiting, or traveling. You can easily solve this problem by buying a foldable potty chair that you can bring with you wherever you go.

Because all potty chairs are somewhat portable, some parents put them in front of the TV, in the kitchen, or in the backyard. However, I don't think this is a good idea. Although you want your child to feel that the elimination process is natural and that it is nothing to be ashamed of, you also want him to understand from an early age that it is not something that is done out in public or in any spot that happens to be convenient. Emphasize the fact that the bathroom is the place where you go when you have to urinate or defecate. You will help your child develop a sense of privacy if you let him follow your example. Every summer at a local pool, I see young mothers setting up their children's potty chairs next to their own lounge chairs. Since the families often spend the entire day at the pool, a child who is toilet training will need his chair, but I can't help feel that it must be uncomfortable for a young trainee to have such a large audience. By all means, take your child's potty chair with you to outdoor activities, but then bring the child and the chair into the public bathroom when it's time to use it. Keeping the potty chair in the bathroom will also help your child concentrate on his toileting needs without being distracted by other things. It's my belief that just as an adult's toilet is always found in the bathroom, so should a child's be.

Some parents worry that if children are trained with a potty chair, they will then have to be retrained to use the toilet. This is not really a problem to worry about. Once children become confident in their toileting abilities, they are most often eager to move on to the big toilet like grownups. However, since your child is still too small to fit comfortably or safely on the adult toilet, you may want to get a child's seat that adjusts to fit over the adult seat. Some of the newer potty chairs are built so that the seat can be removed and then placed on the adult toilet. These dual-use seats are a very practical idea.

Toilet Adapter Seats.

Some children begin their toilet training on toilet adapter seats that fit right on the adult toilet. These seats have an advantage over potty chairs in that they are always used in the bathroom, so a child easily learns where to go when he feels the need to urinate or defecate.

I don't believe, however, that adjustable toilet seats are the best choice at the beginning of toilet training. Most children need help getting on and off these toilet seats, which hampers their growing sense of independence, and this delays the day when the child will be totally responsible for his own toileting needs. Another problem is the fact that when children sit on adult toilets, their feet dangle in the air. This removes the leverage that they need to contract the lower abdominal muscles and push out BMs and puts a strain on the muscles around the anus. So if you buy a toilet seat that fits over the adult seat, you'll also need a footstool for your child to rest his feet on so that his knees are just above his thighs. Or, look for one of the seats that is attached to a stepladder. With the use of the ladder, a child can climb up to the toilet by himself, and then use the rungs as a footrest. (See the illustration on page 44.)

Although the ladder seats solve the problems of independent toileting and dangling feet, many of them still pose a problem because the seats do not fit snugly onto the standard adult toilet—and they generally don't fit at all on padded toilet seats. A loose fit will not put your child in danger, but if, while your child is learning how to use the seat, it should jolt, creak, slip, or in any way move, he may become frightened and you probably won't be able to coax him back onto the toilet for several weeks.

Even if your child likes to sit up on the big toilet and you find a secure seat, keep in mind that some children have fears that have nothing to do with the style of their toilet seat, but rather with the toilet itself. Many children are afraid they will fall into the bowl and be flushed away. If your child expresses this fear, don't just dismiss his belief as nonsense. A child knows that something from his body falls into the bowl and then gets flushed away; how does he know *he* won't? Talk with him, treat his fear seriously, and if he persists in this fear, let him drop a large doll or toy into the bowl so he can watch and see that it will not disappear.

Other children are afraid of the flushing noise a toilet makes. *Always* wait until your child is off the toilet before you flush, and if she is still afraid of the sound, wait until after she leaves the bathroom before you flush. Some children don't mind the sound of a flushing toilet, but may still be upset when you flush because you are discarding something they take great pride in. Many BMs are proudly saved all day until Mom and Dad come home. Everyone gathers around the bowl to applaud and praise; then someone abruptly turns the handle and it's all discarded. Some children feel that their waste product is something to be savored and admired because it is a part of them. If that's the case with your child, don't be so quick to flush. Wait until he is out of the bathroom and distracted with something else; then go back and flush.

If your child wants to use the adult toilet rather than a potty chair, go along with him but make sure the adjustable seat fits securely on the toilet, that he has a secure footrest, and that you don't flush while he is still on the toilet. Although I don't usually recommend starting the training period with these seats, if your child wants to use the big toilet it's best not to fight over it; in the long run, toilet training is easiest when the child is comfortable and happy.

Some children are toilet trained without the use of any kind of special chair or adjustable seat. They are taught to hold themselves over the adult seat by locking their arms straight as they clutch the rim of the seat, or they straddle the seat as they sit backwards and hold onto the tank. Although children have been trained this way, it is not an efficient, safe, or advisable method. The fear of falling, of heights, and of being flushed away are all compounded without a comfortable seat, and the child's feet are not properly supported (even if a foot stool is used), which makes it difficult to pass BMs. Imagine how uncomfortable and insecure you would feel trying to use a toilet with a seat 4 feet off the floor. This is why the right equipment is an important factor in toilet training without tears.

Whether your child uses a potty chair or a toilet adapter seat, your toilet-training efforts will be more successful if you follow these guidelines about the use of toilet-training equipment:

- Do not use the deflector cup because it can easily hurt a child as he gets on or off the seat.
- Do not use restraining straps that may be attached to the seat. Don't leave your child alone when you first begin toilet training, and never force him to sit longer than he wants to. Be aware that the very idea of being tied into the seat may frighten a child and delay his training.
- If your potty chair comes with a tray in front, take it off; it may make a child feel confused. Do not use it to hold food or toys. Although some parents use food, toys, or books as a way to keep their child sitting on the toilet longer, I don't think it's a good idea. Your child needs to know that the potty is for eliminating urine and BMs, not a place to eat or play.
- If your house has several bathrooms, you can either choose to use only one for toilet training, or put the same kind of training equipment in each one.
- Consider letting your child help you pick out and buy his toilet-training equipment. This may make him more willing to use it when you get home.
- Buy the chair or seat at least one week before you expect to begin training so that your child will have time to get used to it. He needs some time to look it over and feel comfortable about using it. Encourage him to spend time sitting on it with all his clothes on just to get used to the feel of it.
- Once your child is comfortable with the chair or seat, explain its purpose. Talk about urine and BMs and cleanliness. Explain that Mommy and Daddy use the big toilet; now he can use the smaller one.

Just as there is no one "right" method of toilet training, or "right" age to begin, there is no one "right" piece of toilet-training equipment. Although I have found the

Imagine how you would feel . . .

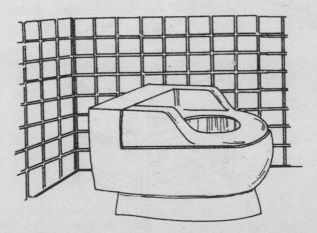

A floor-model potty chair (as described on page 38)

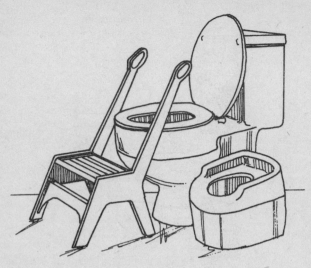

Two models of adaptor seats: (1) a ladder seat, (2) a floor chair with a detachable seat that is made to adapt to an adult toilet.

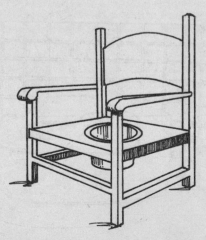

Another standard model potty chair. Note the removable pot.

potty chair illustrated on page 44 to be practical and efficient, you should use whatever makes you and your child most comfortable. There is a list of some available potty chairs and seats in Appendix A to help you choose the one that is right for your child.

Vocabulary

peepee, wiz, wet, number one, pissy, tinkle
poop, poopey, cockey, number two, do-do, duty
bummy, hinney, pussy, twinky, whammer, weiner

Hundreds of words have been invented by parents to describe human waste and the body parts involved in their elimination. Before you begin toilet training, decide what words you will use to talk with your child about urine, bowel movements, penis, vagina, and anus. Many parents use the words that their parents used with them; others use words that neighborhood families use; some use the sounds that their babies use. As you think about what words you will use, keep the following in mind:

- Avoid vague phrases such as, "Do you want to go to the bathroom?" Children can be very literal in their interpretation and say, "No," because they have no interest in going into that particular room in the house. Instead, ask specific questions like, "Do you have to put your BMs or urine into the potty?"
- Use words that the child can say, and yet are as close to "correct" as possible, "Penis," " 'gina" (as in "vagina"), and "anus" are probably not too difficult for your child to pronounce in some way that is near correct. You will run into some trouble, however, if you ask your child to tell you when he has to defecate. Even if a young child tries to say, "I have to defecate," the words probably won't sound like anything meaningful and you'll miss the message. On the other hand, don't use words that are so babyish that you or your child will be embarrassed to say them in public, or one that your child will outgrow. A seven-year-old, for instance, may not tell you he is constipated or has diarrhea be-

cause he's embarrassed to say the word "do-do," and doesn't know what else to call it. In this book I will call bowel movements "BMs" and I will use the word "urine." These are not the only "right" words to use. I've chosen them simply because they are commonly used and easily understood.

- Be consistent. Whatever words you choose to use, stick with them. Don't ask your child in the morning if he has to go tinkle, and then call it peepee in the afternoon, and then tell him not to wet at night. Make sure that other adults who are involved in the care of your child know the words you're using so they will also use them, and will know what your child is saying.

- Make sure the words you use don't imply anything dirty or shameful. Words like "no-no," "messy," "stinky," or "yucky" may give your child the message that you think human waste is disgusting. This attitude can be confusing to a child since you say you want him to pass urine and make BMs, but when he does, you call it a "dirty" name.

It's also important not to state or imply that the child himself is dirty or bad. If you say, "I can smell that you did BMs in your diaper," you acknowledge that BMs smell and that's one way you can tell when a diaper is soiled. This remark gives a very different message than the one a child gets if you say, "You stink." Think before you make any remarks to your child about the elimination process; any negative comment should focus on the behavior, not the child. Phrases like, "You're a mess," can instill guilt in a child and will hurt his self-confidence. It should be rephrased to something more neutral: "BMs can make a mess." The degree of disapproval you show toward your child when he wets or soils his pants depends on the method of toilet training you use, but no matter how severe your tone, you must always make it clear that you disapprove of the behavior, not the child himself.

This rule applies even to the labels of "good boy/bad boy." If a child doesn't use the toilet as you want him to, he is not a bad boy. Even when your child does use the toilet like you want him to, it is better not to say,

"What a good boy!" Equating "good" with using the potty implies that the child is "bad" when he doesn't use it. Even a child who is four or five years old and having difficulty learning mature toileting habits is not bad; although his parents may disapprove of his behavior, the child himself is good.

Finally, it is helpful if your child understands the meaning of "before" and "after." A preliminary lesson in the use of these words will make it easier for your child to understand what you want when you say, "Be sure to tell me you have to make urine before it comes out and wets your diaper."

The vocabulary you use to talk about the elimination process with your child will set the tone of your attitude toward elimination; it will help him understand your specific expectations, and it will help the two of you to communicate openly about something that is as natural and vital as eating and breathing.

Child Care

Carol was shocked the day her two-year-old, Benny, came home from the baby-sitter's and announced, "Mommy, I use my pee-pee. Want to see?" Although Carol was glad that Benny seemed so happy about his new conquest, she was also very angry that the baby-sitter would try to toilet train Benny without talking to her first. Carol is not the first parent to be the last to know that her child is being toilet trained by someone else—someone whose methods and attitudes may be quite contrary to her own.

While you're in the "get set" stage of toilet training, be sure to talk with any other adults who are involved in caring for your child. These people include Grandma, Grandpa, day-care providers, babysitters, and nursery school teachers. It isn't enough just to tell them that your child is learning to use the toilet; if your child will be in their care for any length of time, tell them everything you can that will help them train your child using only the method you have chosen. Tell them what kind of potty chair or seat you're using; what words you use to talk about urine and BMs; the kind of tolerant, calm attitude that you feel is important for toilet training without tears; and even the times of the day when your child should be brought to the bathroom. Then make sure that all the care-givers understand that your child is not to be scolded, embarrassed, or shamed if he has an accident. (Be sure to provide an extra set of clothing every day. If one set gets wet or soiled, he can easily change into dry clothes without any fuss or embarrassment.)

Most people who care for children have well-formed opinions on the various methods of toilet training. So be sure to plan a conference to talk with the people who care for your child before you begin your training period. Make sure that you all plan to use the same method with the same attitude of warmth and tolerance. Chapter Thirteen will give you more details about training with a care-giver.

Teamwork

Years ago it was usually the mother's job to clean the house, cook the food, and raise the children. Today, many parents share these responsibilities, but unfortunately, toilet training is still often the mother's task. As you begin your child's toilet training (whether you're a mom or a dad) take time to make your spouse your partner.

Set aside time to talk about how the two of you will both play a role in the toilet-training process. Make time to read this book together. Read some of it out loud to each other, and share your views on the basic do's and don'ts listed on pages 52-53. It's important that the two of you agree on the ground rules before the training begins. Problems are more likely to occur, for example, if one parent tells the child to use the potty chair, while the other puts him on the toilet, or if one parent insists the child say "bowel movement," and the other says, "ca-ca," or if one parent uses a demanding, scolding approach while the other is patient and understanding.

It was this kind of inconsistent training that turned three-year-old Sharon's training experience into a tearful battle. Sharon's mom, Sue, never ridiculed or scolded Sharon when she wet or soiled her pants. Yet, every time she had an accident, Sharon would cry hysterically, hide in her room, and refuse to have her clothes changed. When Sue told her husband that she didn't understand why Sharon acted that way, Roy was not surprised at all. "She better hide," he said. "If she makes a mess on the nights that I watch her while you're at work, she gets a good spanking from me. That's the only way she'll learn." Roy was usually a tolerant, nurturing parent, so Sue had never even considered that he might be the cause of Sharon's fearful reactions. Sue and Roy had a lot to discuss; they had to find a compromise to their approaches to toilet training so Sharon could look to both of them for consistent guidance. It's best if you and your spouse come to an agreement on the ground rules *before* the training period begins.

Once you and your spouse understand the basic guidelines to use for toilet training without tears and agree on the best approach to use, then you should also agree to share the teaching responsibilities. It helps children to understand the value and importance of mature toileting habits if the learning process is practiced and reinforced by *both* parents. It will also help the child feel secure if he knows his toileting needs can be handled by either parent.

Tracy took total charge of little Jenny's toilet training because she was home with her all day and it seemed the easiest thing to do. Once Jenny was trained, Tracy continued to accompany her to the bathroom to help wipe her clean. This routine worked well until the day when Tracy wasn't home and Jenny had to have a bowel movement. She refused to go alone, and she refused to go with her daddy. She threw herself on the floor in a tantrum and cried until she finally soiled her pants. Without meaning to, Tracy and her husband had taught Jenny that only her mom was allowed to attend to her toileting needs. "I remember I was anxious to wean Jenny from breast-feedings," said Tracy, "so I'd have a little more freedom and my husband could help watch her. Now I still can't get away from the house alone for more than an hour without worrying that Jenny might need me back at home to go to the bathroom. It was a big mistake to let her become so dependent on me." Children need to know that all the adults who love them—Mom, Dad, Grandma, Grandpa, baby-sitters, and such—can help them use the toilet. Once they're trained and able to dress and clean themselves, they can be taught to tend to their own toileting needs.

Dads are usually better than moms when it comes time to teach toddler and preschool boys how to stand up while urinating. Dads who aren't self-conscious about their bodies and bodily functions can let their sons watch how it's done. That's usually all it takes to explain this toileting method. Nancy had been trying for days to explain to three-year-old Danny that he could urinate while he was standing up, but Danny wanted no part of it. His older sister sat on the toilet, his mom sat on the toilet, and the little girl next door sat on a potty, so sitting down was good enough for him. Finally, Nancy asked her husband to let Danny watch him stand while he urinated into the toilet. At first Bob laughed at the idea, but when Nancy persisted, he sheepishly agreed. One time was all it took to convince Danny that he was a big boy who could go pee-pee "just like Daddy."

Make an effort to let toilet training be a team effort by both parents. If your spouse is sometimes away from home on business, schedule the training period at a time when both of you are most likely to be home. If you are separated or divorced, it is still important that both parents be involved in the toilet-training process if at all possible. If the separated parent has any visitation time, he or she will be involved in toileting at some point whether you plan on it or not, so it's best to plan in advance how you will use a consistent method of training. On the other hand, if you're a single parent with no contact with your child's other parent, there is no reason that you alone can't successfully toilet train your child without tears.

You're almost ready to choose the toilet-training method that you think will be best for you and your child. But before you do, use the following questionnaire to check off each aspect of the "ready" and "set" stages of preparation. Then you'll be sure that you understand the guidelines that are basic to all methods of toilet training, and whatever method you use will be one without tears:

Are You Ready?

_____ Have you prepared a positive and warm attitude?

_____ Do you understand your role is one of a teacher, not a drill sergeant?

_____ Do you understand how your child's physiological development affects his ability to toilet train?

_____ Have you begun to develop your child's sensory awareness capabilities?

_____ Have you thought about how you will speak to your child without shame or ridicule when he has a problem?

_____ Have you examined your personal feelings toward human waste, the elimination process, and private body parts so you will give your child the message that they are all a part of a natural, normal body function?

_____ Are you sure you're toilet training your child because you want to, not because of family, social, or personal expectations?

_____ Have you chosen a time for toilet training that will be relatively free of outside obligations, distractions, and stress?

Are You Set?

_____ Have you decided on the kind of equipment you want to use?

_____ Have you established a speaking vocabulary that will be used by all who are involved in the care of your child?

_____ Have you spoken with the people who care for your child while you're away to be sure they use the same equipment, vocabulary, method, and attitude?

_____ Have the gained the committed support of your spouse?

When you've checked off all the preceding blanks, it's time for you to GO.

Read through the rest of this book and choose the method that seems best for you and your child. Then once you have chosen a method, photocopy the following charts of do's and don'ts. Tape them up where you can easily see them, and read them often. They'll remind you of the basic principles of toilet training that have been discussed in this chapter.

DO:

- Develop an attitude that is tolerant, patient, and warm.
- Be calm and casual about toilet training. Treat it as a natural event.
- Educate yourself about the physical aspects of the elimination process so you can be more tolerant of delays and regressions.
- Help your child develop sensory awareness of the elimination process so he can associate the sensations of a full bladder or bowel with the need to urinate or defecate.
- Remember that there is no single "right" age to begin toilet training, nor one "right" method of toilet training.
- Treat your child with respect.
- Expect your child to be curious about his urine and BMs.
- Choose a time for toilet training in which you are not distracted by outside obligations or the stress of new situations.
- Use words to talk about the elimination process that your child can pronounce and that are as close to "correct" as possible.
- Be consistent in your vocabulary use. Choose the words you want to use and then stick with them.
- Make sure all the people involved in the care of your child know how you are toilet training your child.
- Make sure your spouse is your partner in toilet training.

DON'T:

- Don't shout at, shame, or use physical punishment when your child has an accident.
- Don't show strong negative emotions such as anger or disgust when training your child.
- Don't let family or friends pressure you to toilet train with a method or at an age that is not best for you or your child.
- Don't expect your child to train at the exact same age or pace as other children in your family or neighborhood. All children are different in their ability to attain mature toileting habits.
- Don't embarrass your child with ridicule.
- Don't be surprised or shocked if your child plays with or admires the products of his climination efforts.
- Don't use vague phrases like "Go to the bathroom," when you really mean "Put your BMs in the potty."
- Don't use words that imply that the process is "dirty" or "shameful."
- Don't associate moral values with success or failure at toileting, for example, "good" boy if he uses the potty and "bad" boy if he soils his pants. This instills guilt and undermines his self-esteem.
- Don't let anyone involved in the care of your child use punitive training methods.

Chapter Three

The Readiness Approach

The Readiness Approach is the method of toilet training most commonly used in the United States today. It is a relaxed, positive procedure that respects the child's capacity for self-learning and leaves the responsibility for training primarily with the child. Using this method, parents watch for signs that their child is physically, intellectually, and psychologically "ready" to be trained; then they introduce him to the potty chair or toilet seat, and then they wait until he wants to use it. This is not only the most popular method, but it is by far the easiest approach to toilet training.

Determining the age at which a child is ready for this approach, however, is not always so easy. The elimination process is a complex procedure that involves a child's physiological maturity, emotional development, psychological reaction to his parents' attitudes, and an intellectual awareness of elimination sensations and parental expectations. The process of attaining readiness is further complicated by the fact that the child's ability to control his bladder usually does not occur at the same time as the ability to control his bowels. With all of these factors playing a part in your child's state of readiness, the one generalization I can offer is this: Sometime between fifteen months and three years of age, your child will be ready to use the toilet voluntarily. Although such a wide age-range may seem too general to be helpful to you, it should certainly ease your mind about having to hurry into the process or slow down the training pace you may already be caught up in. Despite what your family and friends may say, there is no one "right" age for toilet training. If you want to use the Readiness Approach, put on your detective cap and use the information in this chapter to find out for yourself when your child is ready to be toilet trained.

Physical Readiness

Nighttime bowel control will be your child's first step toward mature toileting habits. This control will usually develop by itself without any effort on your part. You'll notice sometime between nine and twelve months of age that your child's diaper is often no longer soiled when he wakes in the morning. When this happens consistently, you can assume that nighttime bowel control has been attained. Wasn't that easy?

When your child reaches the point of continuous nighttime bowel control, you can begin to look for signs that he is ready to begin daytime bowel and bladder training. The quizzes in this chapter will help you decide when the time is right, but remember, this stage of daytime readiness may not appear for a year or two after nighttime bowel control is established. So be patient and keep your eyes and ears open for the day when your child is ready.

Signs of Physical Readiness

Although there is no clear consensus on exactly when a child's central nervous system is fully able to relay the signals associated with a full bowel and bladder and the need to eliminate, nor when he is physically able to control the sphincter muscles at the openings of the anus and urethra, it is generally believed that a child cannot master complete voluntary control until he is at least eighteen months old. However, a child will probably begin to show signs of the start of voluntary anal muscle control shortly after he learns to walk. Around that time you will notice that his face may redden and that he grunts and strains as he makes an effort to voluntarily push out his BMs. At this point he is learning how to contract and relax the anal sphincter muscle.

This is a good time to help your child develop his sensory awareness of the elimination process. When you see him begin to strain, *don't* jump up, grab him, fling

Watch for clues that your child is ready to start toilet training.

him on the potty seat, and say, "Put those BMs in here."
He will immediately stop bearing down and that will
halt the elimination process completely. Simply call his
attention to what he is doing, give it a name, and give
him an optimistic message, such as: "I see you're doing
BMs in your diaper. Mommy and Daddy do BMs too,
but we put them in the toilet, and someday you will
too." That's enough said for now. If you repeat that kind
of message every time you see him straining, he will
begin to associate the word "BM" and the toilet with
the sensations of elimination.

Introduction of the Potty Chair

You will want to buy a potty chair or toilet adapter
seat during this early stage of physical readiness and put
it in the bathroom. (See page 37 for a full discussion of
potty chairs and seats.) If your child wants to sit on it
while fully clothed, let him. This is a time for getting
comfortable, not for performing. Then in a little while,
you might ask him if he wants to sit on it while he's
naked. Again, do this without any expectation of perfor-
mance; this is still the trying-out period. (Don't ever
force him to sit, or restrain him on the seat in any way.)
Once you decide it's time to begin actual training, then
you'll explain more about its purpose and use.

Modeling

This early stage of readiness is also a good time to
begin modeling. This isn't exactly what it sounds like;
you don't have to strut naked down the bathroom run-
way for your child. This kind of modeling is a method
of training that teaches a child to imitate behavior by
watching a role model. Here are three kinds of modeling
you can use to help your child get ready for toilet
training:

1. Physical modeling: Let your child watch as you, or
   a sibling, or a neighborhood or nursery school
   friend sit on the toilet. Let him hear the noise of
   the urine and BMs; let him see the final result. As
   he's observing, explain that this is where big people
   put their urine and BMs so they don't have to walk

around in wet or soiled pants. Explain that when he wants to try this, you will be happy to help him.

2. Book and video modeling: There are a number of good books about toilet training that are written for children (see Appendix B). As your child watches the pictures and listens to the story of another child who expresses an initial sense of uncertainty about learning to use the potty, he'll feel assured that his hesitant feelings are natural and acceptable. He will also gain courage from the character's eventual success. A story also lets him see the training process from beginning to end.

3. Doll modeling: Use a wetting doll to help your child see how the liquids he drinks become urine that can be deposited into a potty. Some wetting dolls actually come with a potty chair of their own, but if yours doesn't the doll can be placed on your child's own potty. A wetting doll serves a number of purposes: by watching a doll use the potty, your child may develop the attitude, "If she can do it, so can I"; a wetting doll lets your child feel in control of the training situation because he is the one in charge of the doll's training process; as you watch your child train his wetting doll, you'll be better able to determine if he really understands what is expected of him in regard to using the potty. (With a little imagination and some brown clay, you can have the "wetting doll" also do BMs on the potty.)

Timetable of Bowel and Bladder Control

Another sign of physical readiness is the child's development of a regular bowel and bladder routine. This doesn't mean that a child must move his bowels every morning exactly half an hour after breakfast and pass urine 10 minutes after each drink. It means only that if you have some idea of when you can expect your child to defecate or urinate, you'll be able to guide him to the potty at times that are most promising for success. Bowel movements are easiest to track. Some children eliminate every morning after breakfast; others go every day after

Training a doll builds toilet-training confidence in your child

naptime; still others go every other day before bedtime. Use the Patterns of Elimination chart (on page 66) for three to five days to help you keep track of your child's bowel movements. When you look over the chart, you'll be able to see quickly if your child has attained some bowel regularity. The sample chart (on page 60) shows that two-year-old Timmy has achieved a fairly regular pattern of bowel elimination, and it will be easier for his parents to bowel train him if they let him sit on the potty at about 9 A.M. every day.

Readiness for bowel training usually occurs several months before readiness for bladder training. (See page 27 for a full explanation of why this happens.) Therefore, bowel readiness and bladder readiness are two separate aspects of toilet training. This gives you a choice of readiness training strategies: You can concentrate on bowel control alone when you feel your child is ready, or you can postpone starting the training process until your child shows the signs of both bowel and bladder readiness and then begin training for control of both functions at the same time.

PATTERNS OF ELIMINATION

Timmy							
Date:	6/5	6/6	6/7	6/8			
Times:							
7:00 A.M.							
8:00		BM					
9:00	BM		BM	BM			
10:00							
11:00							
12:00 P.M.							
1:00							
2:00							
Continue throughout the day							

I strongly recommend doing bowel training first. It is easier to do and your child's chances for success are greater. Also, urine is released during bowel movements anyway, which helps your child practice the control of the bladder sphincter muscles; once bowel control is attained, bladder control will follow at a natural, easy pace. And finally, if you wait for both bowel and bladder readiness signs to be present before doing any toilet training, you're very likely to find yourself right in the middle of your child's negative phase when it's very difficult to teach him anything.

The last step in the toilet training process is the attainment of nighttime bladder control. For most children this, like nightime bowel control, happens at its own pace without any effort on your part. (See Chapter Twelve for toilet-training strategies for children who are not nighttime bladder trained by age five.) When a child's bladder is mature enough to hold urine for 8 to 10 hours at a time, he will stay dry through the night. You can expect your child to achieve complete nighttime bladder control by age three and a half to four or within one year after attaining daytime bladder control. Although your role in helping him attain nighttime bladder control is usually less active, there are a few things you can do to aid nighttime dryness. These techniques are explained in Chapter Twelve.

Use the following quiz to help you evaluate your child's state of physical readiness. Put a check next to each sign of readiness as your child achieves it. Remember, your child does not have to master every one before you can begin training, but the more he can already do, the easier the training will be.

Physical Readiness Quiz

Daytime Bowel Readiness
My child:
1. has complete nighttime bowel control ____
2. is able to control his anal sphincter muscles (as observed in his ability to bear down and push out BMs, or to postpone the urge to defecate) ____
3. has regular pattern of bowel elimination ____
4. has the manual dexterity to take his pants off and on and to get on the potty seat ____
5. can sit on a chair for 5 minutes ____

Daytime Bladder Readiness
My child:
1. stays dry at least 2 hours between diaper changes ____
2. is dry after a nap fairly regularly ____
3. is able to control his sphincter muscles to postpone wetting ____
4. sometimes wakes up dry in the morning ____

You can hold off training until most signs are evident or you can begin when you see the first signs of readiness. Obviously, the longer you wait, the older your child will be, and the more signs of readiness you see, the faster and easier the training period will be. You can also improve your chances for easy toilet training by considering the intellectual and emotional readiness factors that are also involved in the elimination process. The following sections in this chapter will help you evaluate these areas.

Intellectual Readiness

The age at which a child is ready for toilet training is not related to his IQ (except in the case of retarded and mentally challenged children, whose toilet training is discussed in Chapter Fifteen. However, the ease of toilet training is influenced by a child's intellectual awareness of what's going on in his body, his ability to tell you about it, and his understanding of what you want him to do. Use the following quiz to help you evaluate your child's intellectual readiness. Put a check next to each sign that your child has achieved.

Intellectual Readiness

My child has:
1. shown signs of sensory awareness by:
   —indicating discomfort from soiled or wet diapers   ____
   —recognizing sensations of a full bladder or bowel   ____
   —indicating that he has wet or soiled his diaper by pulling on the diaper or by telling you   ____
   —telling you when he's about to urinate or defecate   ____
2. shown signs of language ability and can communicate the need to defecate or urinate through words or gestures   ____
3. shown that he can follow simple directions like "Sit on this chair" or "Make a grunting noise like I do"   ____
4. shown that he knows what is expected of him during toilet training   ____

Psychological Readiness

Once you determine that your child is physically and intellectually ready for toilet training, you're well on your way to a training experience that will be without tears. One last readiness factor that you should consider before beginning the training period is the state of your child's psychological readiness.

Jane, for example, came to my toilet-training clinic totally frustrated with the entire readiness approach. She had waited until her daughter showed all signs of bowel and bladder readiness before she began the training period, and she knew that Jenny understood exactly what she was supposed to do. Yet, every day they fought when it was time to sit on the potty chair. Not only did Jenny refuse to sit on the potty, but she refused to do anything Jane asked her. "How can I expect to toilet train her," Jane asked, "if I can't even get her to put her socks on in the morning?" The answer was clear: Jenny was in a negative stage of development and was not psychologically ready to do what her mother wanted her to. I have seen many cases like Jane's where, despite an apparent physical and intellectual state of readiness, it would be best to delay toilet training until the child decides she is ready to cooperate, and the parent can see that she is psychologically ready.

The quiz on the next page will help you determine if your child is psychologically ready for toilet training.

The stages of readiness may seem somewhat complex at first as you try to sort bladder readiness from bowel readiness, and physical readiness from intellectual readiness, and all of them from psychological readiness. But if you read through this chapter carefully once again, it will become clear that readiness signs are not difficult to read, and when they are *all* present, the learning process if likely to proceed efficiently and comfortably for both you and your child.

Psychological Readiness

My child:
1. is generally cooperative   _____
2. likes to please her parents   _____
3. understands and enjoys praise   _____
4. is proud of her own accomplishments   _____
5. shows a desire to use the potty   _____
6. tries to imitate her parents or other children
   who use the toilet   _____
7. is interested in cleanliness, order, and putting
   things in their proper place   _____
8. doesn't resort to wild tantrums when in-
   structed to do something   _____

The Method

The method used in the Readiness Approach involves waiting until the child shows signs of readiness, then encouraging and guiding him as he learns bowel control, and then finally helping him master daytime bladder control. You can do this by following these five steps:

1. Set the Stage

Before you even mention toilet training to your child, follow the preparatory guidelines presented in Chapter Two. After you've prepared yourself, your child's caregivers, and your spouse, then you can check for the signs of physical, intellectual, and psychological readiness that are explained in the beginning of this chapter. Once you decide that your child shows enough signs of readiness to begin bowel training, it's time to involve your child in the training process.

2. State Your Expectations

Now it's time to take on the role of the warm and caring teacher. Tell your child in a matter-of-fact way that it's time to use the potty. Explain in simple terms what the potty is for and what you expect your child to do. Be firm, but not demanding, when you say something like, "From now on, I want you to put your BMs in the potty and nowhere else." Point out to your child that Mommy and Daddy (and other older family members) don't use diapers because they put their BMs and urine in the toilet. Explain that now that he's growing up, he too can learn how to use a potty, and soon he won't have to wear diapers anymore. Make sure that you always express confidence in your child's ability to succeed.

3. Plan Out a Daily Practice Schedule

Most children feel more secure and confident when they know what to expect. You can help your child view elimination as one of his natural daily functions by planning a predictable schedule for all his bodily functions, such as eating, exercising, sleeping, and toileting. This will be easier to do for toileting if you have an idea of when your child is most likely to have his bowel movement each day. By charting daily bowel movements for a few days, you should be able to determine the best time of day to bring your child to sit on the potty. (The Patterns of Elimination Chart on page 66 that you used to record bowel regularity during readiness preparation will be of use to you again.)

In the beginning, it's more a matter of your "catching" the bowel movements at the right time than of actual "control" on the part of your child. But the BMs that just happen to land in the pot give a young child a better understanding of your expectations and a feeling of accomplishment that will motivate him to want to do it again. Eventually, your child will be able to hold back his BMs intentionally until he is on the potty and then release them into the bowl.

PATTERNS OF ELIMINATION

Dates:					
Times:					
7:00 A.M.					
8:00					
9:00					
10:00					
11:00					
12:00 P.M.					
1:00					
2:00					
3:00					
4:00					
5:00					
6:00					
7:00					

If your child does not have bowel movements at a predictable time, bring him to sit on the potty every 2 hours throughout the day. You may have a better chance for catching the bowel movement if you watch for bodily signs that indicate a need to defecate and remember that the gastrocolonic reflex most often activates the elimination process 20 to 30 minutes after a meal. (Work with your child's natural elimination schedule; do not use enemas, suppositories, or other laxatives to encourage a bowel movement.)

Choose a day on which your child seems especially happy and agreeable for the first day of potty training. At the appropriate time, lead him to the bathroom and stand by the potty chair. Tell him that you want him to put his BMs into the pot, and then suggest that he sit down and give it a try. If he absolutely refuses to sit on the potty, drop the subject for now and try again in a half hour or so. If he continually refuses to sit on the potty throughout the day, it's a sign that he's not ready for toilet training. Try again in three or four weeks.

If your child does sit on the potty chair, explain again what you want him to do. Sometimes the mere act of sitting on a potty seat causes the sphincter muscles to tighten, so it would be helpful if you squat and grunt as if you were passing BMs and then ask your child to imitate you. This may help his muscles to relax and that will allow his BMs and urine to fall into the pot. Sometimes parents of hyperactive children find it necessary to use toys, games, stories, food, and such to keep their child sitting on the potty. If at all possible, however, try not to get into the habit of potty entertaining. This is not a time for distraction tactics; it's a time to concentrate on the act of elimination.

If your child wants to get up before he's had a bowel movement, let him. Don't plead, beg, or bribe him to stay longer. Just praise him for sitting so nicely. Tell him casually he can try again later and then put his diaper back on. Even if he doesn't mind sitting there, don't drag out the beginning sessions any longer than 5 minutes.

Repeat this procedure every 2 hours until he has his daily bowel movement. Don't be surprised if he has a bowel movement in his diaper almost immediately after getting off the potty. If that happens, he's probably not being defiant; it's likely that his bowel sphincter muscle may tighten when he sits and then it may relax as soon as he stands. To help your child better understand the purpose of the potty, express mild disapproval with a short statement such as, "Oh, your BM should go in the potty, not in your pants." Then take him and the soiled diaper into the bathroom. Empty the contents of the diaper into the potty and calmly explain once again that BMs belong in the pot. Clean the pot and then ask your child to sit on the potty one more time for today. After this practice session, you can let your child sit on the potty again later if he asks to, but otherwise there's no reason to continue the training for the day. Start the schedule again in the morning.

The Readiness Approach: The First Day of Bowel Training

Child's Behavior	Parent's Reaction
Your child at first refuses to sit on potty.	Be matter of fact and try again a little later.
Your child refuses all attempts to toilet train throughout the day.	Stop toilet-training efforts. Try again in 3 to 4 weeks.
Your child sits on potty.	Give an instant reward and record time on the calendar chart (see page 70). Let your child get up anytime he wants.
Your child passes a BM in potty.	Give an instant reward and record date and time on the calendar chart (see page 70); plan to try again tomorrow at the same time.
Your child doesn't pass a BM while on the potty:	Give a reward for sitting on the potty, put the diaper back on with a positive comment, and repeat potty practice every 2 hours until child passes a BM.
Your child passes a BM in his diaper.	Don't scold or punish, but show mild disapproval. Let child watch you empty the BM into the potty. Calmly explain that this is where BMs go. Repeat positive comments, like: "Tomorrow you can put your BM in the potty."

Don't expect much to happen the first few days of training. If your child sits on the potty and understands what you want him to do, you're off to a good start. Stick to the same routine every day, and be patient—it will probably take your child several months to learn complete bowel control. During this time keep track of your child's progress with the Calendar Chart on page 70.

Jeff and Lorraine used the calendar chart shown on p. 71 to keep a record of 22-month-old Melissa's progress and also to reward her successes with stars. They taped the chart to the inside of the bathroom closet door so it was always readily available. Lorraine used the letter "D" to indicate when Melissa soiled her diaper, and she posted a star with the time of day when Melissa successfully put her BMs in the potty. From this chart you can see that in her first month of training, Melissa made slow but steady progress toward voluntary bowel control.

Instructions for the Calendar Chart:

1. Make several copies of page 70 so you can chart your child's progress for a few months.
2. Fill in the days of the month in the appropriate little boxes in each square.
3. Record the time of day each time your child sits on the potty.
4. Write "D" for "diaper" each time your child soils his diapers, and note the time of day.
5. Put a star and the time of day in the box when your child puts his BMs in the potty.

See page 71 for a sample Calendar Chart.

Once bowel control is mastered, you can help your child attain bladder control. Since your child will already be comfortable with the way his sphincter muscle releases urine into the potty at the same time as the BMs, urinating alone should be a simple task to accomplish. When he is able to stay dry for at least 2 hours, lead him to the potty at 2-hour intervals and again after each nap if he wakes up dry. Do not bring him to the potty more often than this. Too many trips to the potty can

THE READINESS APPROACH:
Calendar Chart

SUNDAY	MONDAY	TUESDAY	WEDNESDAY	THURSDAY	FRIDAY	SATURDAY
10/1	10/2	10/3	10/4	10/5	10/6	10/7
Potty Times: 8 AM, Noon, 6 PM — D 9 AM, 9:45 AM	Potty Times: 8 AM, Noon, 6 PM — D 10 AM, D 4 PM	Potty Times: 8 AM, Noon, 6 PM — D 10 AM	Potty Times: 8 AM, Noon, 6 PM — D 9:30 AM	Potty Times: 8 AM *, Noon, 6 PM — D 2 PM	Potty Times: 8 AM, Noon, 6 PM — D 10 AM	Potty Times: 8 AM *, Noon, 6 PM
10/8	10/9	10/10	10/11	10/12	10/13	10/14
Potty Times: 8 AM, Noon, 6 PM — D 9:45 AM	Potty Times: 8 AM *, Noon, 6 PM	Potty Times: 8 AM *, Noon, 6 PM	Potty Times: 8 AM *, Noon, 6 PM	Potty Times: 8 AM, Noon, 6 PM — D 9:45 AM	Potty Times: 8 AM *, Noon, 6 PM	Potty Times: 8 AM *, Noon, 6 PM
10/15	10/16	10/17	10/18	10/17	10/20	10/21
Potty Times: 8 AM *, Noon, 6 PM	Potty Times: 8 AM *, Noon, 6 PM — D 5 PM	Potty Times: 8 AM *, Noon, 6 PM — D 9:45 AM	Potty Times: 8 AM *, Noon, 6 PM	Potty Times: 8 AM *, Noon, 6 PM	Potty Times: 8 AM *, Noon, 6 PM	Potty Times: 8 AM *, Noon, 6 PM
10/22	10/22	10/24	10/25	10/26	10/27	10/28
Potty Times: 8 AM *, Noon, 6 PM	Potty Times: 8 AM, Noon, 6 PM — D 11:45 AM	Potty Times: 8 AM *, Noon, 6 PM — D 3:20 PM	Potty Times: 8 AM *, Noon, 6 PM	Potty Times: 8 AM *, Noon, 6 PM	Potty Times: 8 AM, Noon, 6 PM	Potty Times: 8 AM *, Noon, 6 PM
10/29	10/30	10/31				
Potty Times: 8 AM *, Noon, 6 PM	Potty Times: 8 AM *, Noon, 6 PM	Potty Times: 8 AM *, Noon, 6 PM	Potty Times:	Potty Times:	Potty Times:	Potty Times:

THE READINESS APPROACH:
Calendar Chart

SUNDAY	MONDAY	TUESDAY	WEDNESDAY	THURSDAY	FRIDAY	SATURDAY
Potty Times:	Potty Times:	Potty Times:	Potty Times:	Potty Times:	Potty Times:	Potty Times:
Potty Times:	Potty Times:	Potty Times:	Potty Times:	Potty Times:	Potty Times:	Potty Times:
Potty Times:	Potty Times:	Potty Times:	Potty Times:	Potty Times:	Potty Times:	Potty Times:
Potty Times:	Potty Times:	Potty Times:	Potty Times:	Potty Times:	Potty Times:	Potty Times:
Potty Times:	Potty Times:	Potty Times:	Potty Times:	Potty Times:	Potty Times:	Potty Times:

be counterproductive because they do not help him learn to hold back his urine.

After attaining bowel control, bladder control is an easy concept for most children to grasp, so you probably won't need to renew the reward system (see below) or the daily progress chart, but you certainly can if you or your child wants to. Just be sure to remind your child every 2 to 3 hours that it's time to put urine in the potty. Don't try to avoid wetting accidents by reducing your child's fluid intake. This is not a good idea for a number of reasons:

- You are trying to teach your child to hold back urine until he is on the potty. Restricting fluids will not help you reach this goal.
- Fluids are part of your child's basic daily needs. If you are unresponsive to this thirst, you will make him angry, not toilet trained.
- It won't work.

A restriction of fluids concentrates the urine, making the need to urinate more, not less, urgent. If your child is ready to be bladder trained, a sensible daily schedule of going to the potty at 2-hour intervals will do the job.

Eventually, as your child gains voluntary control, you'll be able to cut down on the number of trips to the potty because he will tell you when he has to go. Then once bowel and daytime bladder control are fully established, your child will be able to assume complete responsibility for remembering to keep dry and clean.

4. Motivate Your Child

The Readiness Approach to toilet training is based on your child's ability and willingness to achieve mature toileting habits. Although the ultimate success of the training depends on his readiness, you should make a consistent effort to motivate him to cooperate. Right from the start, you can do a lot to help him maintain his desire to use the potty and to foster his feelings of personal pride by encouraging and rewarding any effort toward toilet training. The simple act of pulling down his pants by himself or sitting on the potty seat are signs of cooperation that should be acknowledged regardless of the outcome. As the training sessions continue and your child becomes used to the potty routine, the motivating devices can be saved for when he actually puts BMs in the pot.

There are two different ways to motivate your child. One way is with rewards that are given after the desired action is completed. Make sure you have the rewards handy for immediate feedback. Rewards that are delayed until you can get to the store have no positive reinforcing effect because children are unable to make the connection between a morning behavior and an afternoon treat. The second type of motivating devices are those that are offered to prompt the child to do what you want before the desired act is attempted.

Rewards

- The best reward you can give to your child is consistent praise, but don't overdo it. Since you want to emphasize the "natural" aspect of elimination, and since you do intend to eventually dispose of the products of elimination, it is probably best not to react with hurrays or alleluias, nor is it necessary to engage banners or brass bands. A warm smile, a hug, and a few kind words when your child uses the potty are all that's necessary to let him know that you are pleased with his progress. Make sure you praise your child's efforts every time he goes into the bathroom. Even if he changes his mind and won't sit down when you get there, even if he interrupts your phone conversation and then has nothing to put in the potty, even if you rush home from shopping only to find it's too late, even then, make sure you always find something nice to say about his intentions.
- Although words of praise are enough to motivate some children, others need something concrete to encourage their training; the most commonly used material rewards are edible treats. Stock your bathroom cabinets with treats that your child likes, such as raisins, candies, or cookies. Make sure that these

treats are not available to him at other times of the day; keep them out of his reach, and make sure he knows they're for successful toileting efforts. It might sound nice to offer a trip to the ice cream store as a reward for putting BMs in the pot, but it's not an effective motivator since the reason for the ice cream will be forgotten by the time you get there.

- Many children are proud to wear sticker rewards. You can buy full pages of brightly colored stickers (the kind teachers sometimes put on the top of the school papers) that have happy faces or cartoon characters on them. These stickers are nice rewards because when your child wears one on his shirt, he is constantly reminded of his toileting efforts.

  You can also get stickers or stars to put on the calendar chart you've taped to the back of your bathroom door. These will help you keep track of your child's progress, and your child will be pleased to see the stars as they increase in number over time.

- You can offer toys as rewards if you like, but they have a few drawbacks. It gets expensive to keep up this reward system; they're hard to hide out of sight in the bathroom, and when you run out of toys, a few raisins will no longer be effective motivators. If your child is over two years of age, you might try offering a reward system in which you agree to buy a desired toy when your child gets three stars in a row on the calendar chart. This kind of long-term motivator can help an older child take more responsibility for his toileting needs.

Prompts

Things that prompt a child to want to use the potty are often used very early in the training process. When you buy the potty chair and place it next to the grown-up's toilet, for example, you are prompting your child to want to give up diapers. The modeling techniques described on page 57 are also methods of prompting that can encourage a child to want to learn bowel and bladder control.

When your child is ready for bladder-control training, you can then also prompt him to use the potty by offering him training pants. These pants have two practical uses in toilet training: They give children a clear message that says using the potty is a grown-up activity that will bring them out of "baby" diapers, and it is very uncomfortable to walk around in "big boy" or "big girl" pants that are wet or soiled. A desire for cleanliness may encourage a child in training pants to use the potty.

Training pants look like regular underwear, but they are padded to be more absorbent if and when accidents happen. (A list of several manufacturers of training pants may be found in Appendix A.) Make sure the training pants are loose enough so your child can take the responsibility of pulling them down and then back up. If your child is over 40 pounds, you may have to make your own training pants by sewing a cloth diaper into a regular pair of underwear. Some parents are making their own training pants in this way even for smaller children because they've found that although the new cartoon character underwear is a great motivator, it's a little too messy for children in training. A piece of cloth diaper tacked into the crotch solves the problem, and prompts their children to trade in their diapers for the colorful underpants.

Once you start to use training pants, it's best to use them throughout the day. If your child has an accident, clean him up and put on another pair of training pants. It will seem like punishment if you put him back into diapers every time he wets or soils. It is also counterproductive to make a child stay in wet or soiled pants to "teach him a lesson." Once your child is in training pants you'll have to carefully schedule your trips to the store and to visit friends. If you wait to use training pants until after bowel control has been attained and bladder readiness signs are evident, it shouldn't be too difficult to leave the house at some time during the day without too much worry. But since you want to spare your child the embarrassment of a public accident, and you don't want to put him in and out of diapers all day, you will have to plan ahead before you leave home.

Since most children are not ready for nighttime bladder control until after they master daytime bladder control, you should put the diaper back on your child at night. Children who are proud of their "grown-up" underwear may resist this return to diapers, so be prepared to explain patiently that when children sleep their urine sometimes leaks out without them even knowing it; so it's okay to wear a diaper at night. If you notice your child is occasionally waking up dry in the morning, you may want to put a plastic liner on the mattress and let him wear his training pants to bed. Just remember, however, that wet sheets in the middle of the night are to be expected, and that you should stay with the diapers until your child consistently wakes up dry if it's going to make you angry to change them.

5. Teach Your Child to Signal

When your child becomes accustomed to using the toilet and you have settled into a routine toileting schedule, you can further promote independent toileting by teaching your child to signal to you when he has to go.[1] You can do this in the following manner:

- Talk to your child about what he is doing every time you take him to the bathroom. Say to him, "It's time to go to the potty." Then invite him to say it back to you by asking a question like, "What time is it now?"
- When he is ready to leave the bathroom, ask him again what he just did. If your child can't answer you with the word "potty," tell him and then ask him again. Continue asking and supplying the answer until he can answer you. Do this every time you take him to the bathroom. When he can answer without any prompting from you, he understands the meaning of the word.
- Whenever your child answers you correctly, reward him with your approval and praise. Eventually he will learn to signal his need to go to the bathroom without any prompting from you.

As you begin the Readiness Approach to toilet training, you'll find yourself very much involved in the process. You'll work in advance of the training to set the stage; then you'll explain your expectations; then you'll set a practice schedule and bring your child to the potty every day and encourage him to use it; then you'll offer rewards for even the slightest hint of cooperation and effort. And you'll keep track of your child's progress on the calendar chart.

Once you've set the training into motion, however, it will be time to watch for opportunities to give increasing responsibility for toileting to your child. The goal in toilet training is to have your child develop independent toilet habits, so as you go along, give only as much help as is needed. Let your child pull down his own pants; let him get on the potty by himself; let him get off and pull up his pants himself. When he's able, let him practice wiping himself clean, let him dump the contents of the potty into the toilet, and let him use a step stool by the sink to wash and dry his hands. More details about teaching good hygiene are in Chapter Six.

Throughout the training process, work to phase out the number of times you have to remind your child to use the potty, the number of rewards you offer, and then eventually, even your presence in the bathroom. As your child gains toileting proficiency, it should not be necessary for you to continue the job of offering rewards for going to the bathroom, of accompanying him into the bathroom, or of wiping him clean. As you venture into the toilet-training process with the Readiness Approach, keep in mind that your goal is to work your way completely out of your child's toileting routine.

The Readiness Approach: Problems and Solutions

Problems	Solutions
Your child refuses to use the potty.	Stop toilet training for 3 to 4 weeks.
After training has begun your child has occasional accidents.	Show mild disapproval, clean up the mess without any fuss, and give a supportive message.
Your child becomes ill during the toilet-training period.	Discontinue training until your child is physically well.

Problems	*Solutions*
Your child was bowel trained, but then begins to soil his pants; he may find a hiding place, such as a corner, to go in private.	Consider causes of soiling such as illness, new sibling, etc. Stress will often show itself in toileting regression. If there are no apparent stress factors, then accept regression as a part of toilet training. Whether stress related or not, don't become angry or show severe disappointment. This may cause further regression. Renew your original training process. If bowel control is not resumed after 2 weeks of a calm retraining routine, stop all training efforts. Express understanding, put the child back into diapers again until he shows a desire and commitment to use the potty.
Due to constipation, the child experiences painful straining while on the potty, and he is reluctant to use the potty again.	Matter-of-factly continue the training with regular visits to the potty. Prevent constipation in the future with a sensible diet that includes roughage (whole-grain cereals, wheat bread, fresh fruit); provide time for adequate exercise and play, and maintain a relaxed attitude to avoid anxiety that may bind up a child's excretory system.

The Advantages of the Readiness Approach

- It is the easiest method to implement.
- It does not pressure a child to train.
- It is the method least likely to cause your child emotional upset.
- It is the most popular method and the one most familiar to parents.
- It is the method most often endorsed by child development experts.

The Disadvantages of the Readiness Approach

- Your child may be physically ready at the same time that he is in the "terrible twos." This may cause him to resist any efforts at toilet training.
- This approach cannot be hurried. You must follow your child's pace, not your own schedule.
- Parents may misread the signs of readiness and try to train before their child is really ready.

Do's and Dont's of the Readiness Approach

DO:
- Set the stage for toilet training by letting your child get used to seeing the potty chair in the bathroom.
- Provide a model. Let your child observe another child or you using the toilet. Read stories to your child about other children who are learning how to use a potty seat. Let your child "train" a wetting doll.
- Observe your child for the signs of physical, intellectual, and psychological readiness.
- Use the Patterns of Elimination Chart on page 66 to find your child's elimination schedule.
- Begin toilet training with bowel-control readiness.
- Have regularly scheduled times for toileting.
- Be calm and casual about the training.

- Encourage your child to develop a regular time-table for all bodily functions, including eating, exercise, sleeping, and toileting.
- Be sensitive to your child's feelings of fear, embarrassment, and pride.
- Expect your child to be successful.
- Remind your child when it's time to sit on the potty.
- Give immediate and consistent rewards for cooperation and successes.
- Begin training for bladder control when your child masters bowel control and shows signs of bladder-control readiness.
- Encourage bladder control by putting your child in training pants.
- Associate toileting with independence and growing up.
- Give prime responsibility for control and cleanliness to your child.
- Be patient.
- Expect occasional regression.
- Stick to your daily toileting schedule as long as your child is willing.
- Include in your toileting routine the habit of washing hands after using the potty.

DON'T:
- Force training on your child if he strongly resists it.
- Shout at, shame, or use physical punishment when your child has an accident.
- Use restraining straps on the potty chair.
- Make the child sit on the toilet for more than a few minutes.
- Let your child play or eat while sitting on the potty.
- Expect too much too soon.
- Overdo your praise when your child successfully uses the potty.
- Use enemas, suppositories, or other external aides.

Chapter Four

The Early Approach

The Method

The Early Approach is a method of toilet training that can be used to bowel and bladder train children who are between three months and fifteen months of age. Using this method, parents initially make a daily habit of placing their children on a potty seat in an effort to "catch" their BMs and urine. Over time, children who are trained with this method become conditioned to associate the feel of the potty on their buttocks with the need to urinate or defecate and they respond by eliminating when they are placed on the potty. Eventually, they even begin to reach or grab for the potty as a signal to their parents that they are holding back their urine and/or BMs until they are placed on the potty.

Although the Early Approach is a valid and plausible method of teaching toileting skills, as you prepare to use this approach, you may need to redefine what is meant by the term "toilet training." With other methods of training, the parents' goal is to teach the child mature and independent toileting habits. It is expected that by the end of the training period, the child will be able to hold back his BMs and urine for a considerable length of time, get on and off the toilet alone, get undressed and dressed alone, and gain complete voluntary bowel and bladder control. This cannot be your immediate goal in the Early Approach, however, because most children do not develop complete voluntary control over the sphincter muscles of the rectum and bladder until after they are fifteen months old. So the goal in early training is not to attempt to make children completely responsible for their elimination functions, but rather to condition them to eliminate urine and BMs only when they feel the potty under their buttocks, and to signal their toileting needs to their parents by reaching or grabbing for the potty.

These two conditioned reflexes can be taught to young children through association. This is a method of learning in which a person is repeatedly exposed to two conditions at the same time so that he learns to associate one condition with the other. Then when one condition is presented, he will automatically respond with the second. The classic example of learning through association is the case of Pavlov's dogs, who were consistently given their food at the sound of a ringing bell. After a period of time the dogs would salivate in expectation of their food as soon as they heard the sound of the bell. Reflex conditioning caused these animals to respond physically to a particular stimulus. Reflex conditioning can also effectively bring babies to physically respond to the daily routine of toileting with a potty.

You have probably already observed how children learn things through association. Newborns quickly learn to associate the smell and sounds of their parents with care and comfort. It's been observed that if you play the same music to a sleepy infant at bedtime, he or she is likely to show signs of sleepiness when you play the same music on subsequent nights. At three months of age, some infants will make visible signs of anticipation (such as kicking, coughing, or smiling) when they see their bottle being prepared; this is because they have come to associate the bottle with the satisfaction of their hunger. Babies as young as four to six months of age often amaze their parents with how much they know through association:

"Every time I put my coat on the baby cries for me," said one mother. "How does she know I'm going out?"

"If the baby hears the stairs creak as I walk up, he jumps up in his crib and starts to cry for me to pick him up," said another parent. "How does he know the creaking sound means somebody's out there?"

"My baby is so smart," a new father said, grinning. "When I took out my tennis racquet the other day, she crawled over to give me the tennis ball she plays with. How can she know the two go together?"

The answer to all these parents' questions is: conditioning through association. This is also the method by which a child can be toilet trained at a young age.

Although the Early Approach to toilet training does not teach children totally independent toileting skills, it does train them to recognize the feel of the potty under their buttocks, to respond by relaxing the sphincter muscles in their rectum and bladder, and it eventually teaches them to hold back their urine and BMs and signal to be put on the potty. If you would like to teach your child to do this, follow the steps in the next section.

Step One: Prepare Yourself

Before you toilet train your child with the Early Approach, you should prepare yourself for the training in the ways discussed in Chapter Two. Then read the additional information in this preparatory section. It will help prepare you more specifically for using the Early Approach.

Attitude

Before beginning the Early Approach, you should pay particular attention to preparing your attitude; it is a key factor in determining how successful your early training program will be. The Early Approach is a very slow working method that will take several months to complete. Throughout this time, you'll need to remain supportive, warm, patient, and accepting of the individual pace of your child's progress.

It is sometimes easy to forget the importance of a proper attitude when working with infants, because it seems they are unaware of our feelings. But, in fact, infants have acute sensory perceptions. They do not need a vocabulary to sense their parents' negative attitudes. They observe it in things like muscular tension, tone of voice, and facial expressions. You will not be able to hide your anger or disappointment from your infant, so take some time to examine your feelings before you begin. The following historical and cultural discussion of the early approach to toilet training will give you a better understanding of the importance of a warm and straightforward attitude during this kind of training program.

An early approach to toilet training was the standard method used in America in the 1920s and 30s. Like the Early Approach outlined in this chapter, this approach was also a conditioning method based on learning by association. In parental attitude, however, it was quite different. Parents in the 1920s were coerced by child development experts and pediatricians into believing that an early approach to toilet training (by three months at the latest) was the only correct way to train children. These parents were given strict instructions on the implementation of a harsh and rigid regime. Children were passive recipients of this daily routine that involved conditioning their rectum with a soap stick and putting the child on the pot each day after the morning and evening bath, "not varying the time by as much as five minutes."[1] This method was practiced in a stern, punitive manner without any display of parental warmth or understanding.

This method of early training fell from popularity when psychoanalytic studies suggested a relationship between this kind of early training and later emotional maladjustment and psychological problems. Even today, parents often express the fear that the Early Approach will in some way traumatize their children. After years of analytic and cross-cultural studies, however, we now know that the age at which a child is trained is not the cause of later emotional and psychological problems; rather, it is the parental attitude that is used during the training period that will determine the long-term effect of toilet training.

A number of cross-cultural studies have found that the Early Approach to toilet training is the standard method of training in other countries. Many of these people have successfully used an early method to teach their children both bowel and bladder control, and they have done it for many years without any evidence of later emotional problems. The Digo people of East Africa, for example, begin toilet training their young at two or three weeks of age. The children are able to urinate on command in a trained position by at least four or five months of age, and they attain complete bowel control by one year.[2] The Digo method differs from the 1920s American early method in two ways: The Digo child is encouraged to be an active, rather than passive, participant in the training routine, and the training is consistently done with a nurturing and responsive attitude that focuses on the child's individual needs and elimination schedule. An early approach conducted with this same kind of gentleness and care is also used in the People's Republic of China. There bladder and bowel control is commonly reported to be accomplished by eighteen months of age.[3]

If you decide to use the Early Approach to toilet training, prepare to bring your child to the potty as part of your daily routine, like washing his face and giving him food. Don't let it become a big deal or a source of conflict between you and your child. This method seems to work best with children who have a calm and easygoing personality. Children who are hyperactive or difficult may find it too stressful to make toileting a part of their daily routine right now. The program is also not recommended for children who are developmentally delayed in their learning abilities. If you and your child feel comfortable using the Early Approach, that's fine. If either one of you doesn't respond well to it, that's okay, too. You can try again a few weeks later, or you can wait to use another method at a later time. In any event, it's your attitude that will be a most important factor in toilet training your child.

Motive

There are many reasons for using the Early Approach. Some are valid ones; whereas some others are not. Before you begin early toilet training, examine your motives. Some *valid* reasons for using the Early Approach include:

- You feel your child will respond well to this kind of conditioning.
- You see this as a way to keep your child clean and to eliminate the times when he might otherwise sit in soiled diapers and risk irritating diaper rashes.
- You have the time and the patience to use this approach and you're curious to observe how it works.
- You want to encourage an awareness of proper toileting habits before your child reaches the negative stage in the "terrible twos."
- You feel that daily toileting will reduce the cost and the bother of keeping your child in diapers.
- You plan eventually to put your child in a day-care facility that requires the children to be toilet trained, and you believe this Early Approach will be a good way to improve the chances that he will be trained by the time you plan to enroll him.

Invalid reasons for using the Early Approach include:

- You want the admiration of family and friends who will think you and your child are wonderful if he can be fully trained by his first birthday.
- You're tired of changing diapers.
- Someone else (your mother, mother-in-law, your spouse, etc.) insists it's the best method to use.
- You want to keep up with your neighbor who claims her toddler slept through the night at one month and was fully toilet trained at one year.
- You want your child to excel in everything. Early toilet training will be one more way to certify his "superbaby" status.

It's important to examine your motives for choosing the Early Approach because your motive will often affect your attitude. If you're pushed into a method or choose it for purely selfish reasons, it is unlikely that you will be able to maintain an attitude and a home atmosphere that is understanding, warm, and accepting.

With the wrong motive and wrong attitude, the early method will be difficult and frustrating for both you and your child.

Principles of Physical Development

As you check your attitude toward early training and examine your motives for using this approach, you can also prepare for the training period by learning more about the physical development of your infant.

In Chapter Two you read about the principles of physical development that affect a child's ability to be completely toilet trained. Because of the course of maturation, the goal of early conditioning cannot be the mastery of total voluntary bowel and bladder control before fifteen months of age. The early process does, however, also work along with the progressive stage of infant's physical development.

A newborn's first bowel movements are a sticky, dark, tarlike matter called meconium, which is built up in his system before birth. Then in a few days, the stools turn watery and change to a yellowish-brown color. These movements are frequent and sporadic during the first few weeks. In the first month, breast-fed babies usually have a bowel movement during or after each feeding—an average of six each day. These stools are often loose and unformed with a very mild odor. Bottle-fed babies also have loose stools, but they are passed less frequently and have a stronger odor.

By four weeks of age the number of daily bowel movements usually drops to three or four each day, and they usually occur upon waking and after eating. By eight weeks of age, the average infant will have two bowel movements daily, one upon waking and one near or during a feeding. Then by sixteen weeks, signs that a BM is imminent are often apparent in the way that the baby turns red, becomes suddenly quiet and still, grunts, and so on.

Newborns urinate 20 to 30 times a day until they are two or three months old. In the following few months, the frequency of urination decreases, while the volume of each elimination increases. By twenty-eight weeks of age, the infant may stay dry for 1- to 2-hour intervals.

While the very young infant's BMs and urine are passed frequently and are generally unpredictable, their elimination is also entirely involuntary. The gastrocolonic reflex causes the infant's anal and urethral sphincter muscles to relax automatically, which allows for immediate, unpredictable, frequent, and unformed elimination. This is obviously not a good time to begin toilet training. But at approximately three months of age an infant begins to pass well-formed stools, and is able to retain his urine and BMs for more predictable periods of time. At this time the infant also becomes aware of the sensations of elimination and is ready to begin the Early Approach to toilet training.

When training children under 15 months of age, the goal is to condition them to hold back their BMs and urine, and then to relax the sphincter muscles and release their waste products when they feel the potty seat under them. Although it is not known exactly when a child can attain this kind of muscular control, studies have shown that some infants between three and six months can learn this skill very successfully, provided their care-giver is observant of the signs that indicate a need to eliminate and then acts promptly to put the child on the potty. Later you'll learn how to work with your child's natural elimination schedule during the Early Approach to toilet training.

Equipment

Once you decide to use the Early Approach to toilet training, you'll need to get the necessary equipment. If you use disposable diapers, make sure to buy the kind that have refastenable tabs. It is less expensive and easier to reseal the old diaper after each trip to the potty than it will be if you have to use a new diaper each time. If you use cloth diapers, be sure your pins are new and easy to use; the pin should be sharp enough to slip easily in and out of the diaper.

You will also need some type of potty seat. If you are training a child who cannot yet sit alone for 5 minutes (this generally applies to children under eight months of age), you will need a lap pot. Unfortunately, you can't buy a pot made specifically for early toilet training, so you'll have to use a bit of ingenuity to find one that fits this purpose. You are going to place this pot on your lap between your legs, and you will hold your child as he sits on it. Therefore, your pot:

- Should be just a bit larger than the size of your child's buttocks.
- Should not be made of soft plastic (like a Tupperware bowl), because, in time, soft plastic will stain and retain the smell. (The pot may be made of ceramic or glass, but porcelain, metal, or a hard plastic are preferable because they won't break if they fall on the floor.)
- Should have a lip around the edge of the bowl so that it will not easily fall through your lap onto the floor.
- Should not have any sharp edges.

The illustration on the next page shows a picture of a pot; this will give you an idea of what your lap pot should look like. (Some parents use the removable bowl that comes with a potty chair; they say it's just right for the job.)

Before you actually begin the Early Approach, you should decide how you will hold your child over the lap pot. One mother who has used the Early Approach successfully to train her three sons, one of them retarded, recommends the following procedure:

1. Make a habit of setting the lap pot and some toilet tissues next to you each time you sit down to give your child a feeding.
2. Undo the left side of the child's diaper.
3. Place the child's head in your left arm and offer him the bottle or breast. (If you are left-handed, you may feel more comfortable placing your child's head in your right arm.)
4. The moment you observe that your child is about to have a BM, take the diaper off by reaching under him and pulling the diaper away from the buttocks.
5. Place the pot between your legs and place your child's buttocks over it. (Leave the diaper across

the child's front, especially if it is a boy, to protect yourself from being sprayed.)

6. Lean your baby back on your arm and continue feeding.
7. Leave the baby on the pot until he's finished feeding.
8. If your baby has passed a BM, use the toilet tissue to clean him and then refasten his diaper.
9. If the feeding is finished and he has not passed a BM, refasten his diaper in a relaxed manner.

This mother found this method worked very well for all her children. She reported that the babies did not show signs of any discomfort, nor did the procedure disrupt their feeding schedules.[4]

This method of holding will work well with most infants. As your child gets a bit older and has his bowel movements at times other than while feeding, you will have to watch throughout the day for his body signals of elimination. When you see him prepare to defecate, put the pot between your knees, undo one side of the diaper and pull it clear of his buttocks, and then sit him upright on the lap pot facing forward with his back to your belly.

If you are using the Early Approach to toilet training

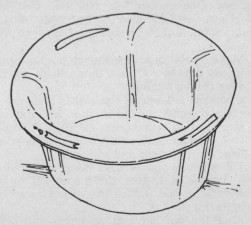

A lap pot for use in early training

with a child who can sit on his own for 5 minutes (generally children over eight months old), then you can use a standard potty chair. (Do not use a toilet adapter seat for such young children.) Make sure the potty chair is sturdy and stands securely on the floor. Do not use the deflector cup, because it may hurt your baby if he scrapes against it as you put him on or take him off the seat. Do not strap your baby into the seat; this feels too confining, and you will never leave him alone anyway. At first, you will probably be unable to explain clearly to your child the reason for sitting on the potty chair, so you might use a few toys, books, or edible treats to encourage him to sit there.

Observation Period

Before you actually begin toilet training your child, set aside a few days just to watch him for bodily signs of elimination. In the beginning of the training period, your child will not be able to tell you when he has to eliminate, so you must learn the signals he gives out as he prepares to urinate and defecate. As previously mentioned, such signals include grimaces, a flushed face, increased body unrest, straining, grunting, and quieting. Every time you change your baby's diaper, test yourself: Did you know the diaper would be wet or soiled? Did you see your child prepare to eliminate? Did you watch his bodily signs as he passed his urine or BMs?

Use the Patterns of Elimination Chart on page 92 to keep track of your child's soiled diapers during this observation period. This will help you determine if your child has a set routine of elimination and when it is most likely to occur. Close observation of your child's body signals and elimination schedule will continue to be important as you use the early method.

The Early Approach
Patterns of Elimination Chart

Dates:					
Times:					
7:00 A.M.					
8:00					
9:00					
10:00					
11:00					
12:00 P.M.					
1:00					
2:00					
3:00					
4:00					
5:00					
6:00					
7:00					

Step Two: Elimination Conditioning

The goal of Elimination Conditioning in the Early Approach is to establish a close relationship between your baby's body signals and his defecation on the potty.

During this part of the training, use the following procedure every day. (This procedure and those subsequent steps are adapted from an article titled, "Shaping Self-initiated Toileting in Infants."[5]

- Keep the potty within 2 to 5 feet of your baby whenever possible.
- When you observe a body signal, hold or tap the potty so your child pays attention to it.
- Hold your baby over the potty in the way you've decided is most comfortable for both of you.

- If your child has already passed the BMs in his diaper when you pick him up, do not place him on the potty. This will confuse the conditioning objective of associating the feel of the potty seat with the sensations of elimination. In order for learning through association to occur, your baby must feel the pot under his buttocks within 2 seconds after he initiates a bowel movement.
- If your child defecates or urinates within about 3 minutes of being held over the potty, show pleasure and approval by hugging, kissing, singing, or presenting objects he will like.
- If he does not eliminate in this time period, put his diaper back on and return him to the activity he was previously involved in.
- If your child eliminates in his diaper, quickly and impersonally change the diaper without showing any signs of anger, disapproval, or disappointment.

It is impossible to remember day after day when your child urinated, when he defecated, when he used the potty, when he went in his diapers, and when and what kind of body signals he gave. The Early Approach Record form on page 94 will help you keep track of these things. While you're using the chart for Step Two, however, ignore the section on this form entitled "Reaching/Grabbing." You will use that section when you move on to the next step, after your child has a minimum of 18 defecations on the potty, and 8 out of 10 consecutive training days are without bowel accidents.

It is difficult to determine how long it will take for your child to meet these criteria. It depends on many factors, including your commitment to the method, the consistency of training, your ability to observe body signals, and your child's personality. The results of a recent study of four infants who were trained with the Early Approach will give you a general idea of time: The study found that the oldest child who began the program at five months and four weeks of age completed Step Two in 36 days, whereas the youngest child who began the method at three months and one week of age finished

THE EARLY APPROACH RECORD

Date/Time	Potty		Diaper/Pants		Body Signals	Reaching/Grabbing
	BM	Urine	BM	Urine		

this step in 19 days.[6] Plan to spend about one month working with the procedure outlined in Step Two.

Step Three: Self-initiated Toileting

The goal of Step Three is to establish a relationship between the child's need to eliminate and his reaching or grabbing for the potty.

When you have completed Step Two of the training method, continue to keep the potty within 5 feet of your child as often as possible, but now make sure it is always placed in front and to the right of him. Then follow these procedures:

- When your baby signals, help him grab for the potty by taking his hands and helping him reach for the potty and then place him on it.
- Continue to use the Early Approach Record form on page 94, adding your child's attempts to reach or grab for the potty.
- Place the baby on the potty anytime he reaches or grabs for the potty without being prompted to do so by you.
- If your baby neither reaches for the potty on his own, nor shows any body signals, help him grab for the potty and then place him on it whenever he is expected to urinate (based on your Patterns of Elimination Chart, or after a feeding or a nap, or after a period of 30 to 65 minutes with no urinations).
- Gradually reduce the number of times you prompt your child to reach for the potty until he will reach or grab when you simply call his attention to it.

You should halt this procedure when your child reaches or grabs for the potty more than half the times that he eliminates over a week's period of time, providing that in this same period the baby does not soil or wet his diaper more than once out of every 10 eliminations. It is important to note if the reaching response is followed by elimination on the potty, because in the beginning of the training period you may find that approximately half of the reaching/grabbing responses will be false alarms that are not yet related to a need to urinate or defecate, but rather to an interest in this new object.

As in Step Two, the amount of time it takes to complete Step Three depends on many factors. The study cited in Step Two found that the child who was five months old when the training began took 38 days to complete this step, whereas the three-month-old took 72 days. Based on these numbers, you should expect to spend about two months in Step Three.

Step Four: Reinforcement

During Step Four, you will no longer need to keep a record of body signals, because the goal here is to phase out your involvement in prompting your child to reach for the potty and to bring him to reach for it himself consistently whenever he feels the need to use it. (You should, however, continue to keep a record of his potty times and reaching/grabbing efforts.) The procedure for Step Four is as follows:

- Put your child in training pants or underwear during the day so that you can easily see if he wets or soils without frequently opening his diaper.
- Increase the distance between your child and the potty to somewhere between 2 and 15 feet.
- Continue to praise all reaching/grabbing efforts.
- Call your baby's attention to the potty when you anticipate that he may wet or soil his pants, but keep the number of daily prompts to a minimum.

To determine when your child is finished with Step Four and therefore may be considered fully trained with the Early Approach, you'll need to keep accurate notes on the Early Approach Record Form. You can end the procedures of Step Four when:

1. Fifteen out of 18 consecutive days pass without your child soiling or wetting his pants.
2. You have given no more than one prompt a day to urge your child to use the potty.
3. During the 15 days without soiling or wetting, your

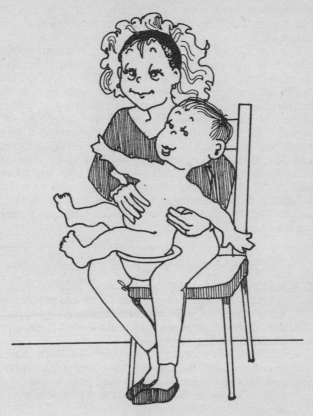

A comfortable training situation for baby and mother.

child eliminated 80 percent of the times when he reached for the potty.

Again, the time required to complete this step varies. The child cited earlier who began the procedure at five months and four weeks of age completed step Four in 20 days, which brings his total time of toilet training to 95 days (approximately three months and one day), whereas it took the younger child who began the training procedure at three months and one week of age 2 days to complete Step Four, which brings his total time of training to 116 days (approximately three months and six days).

The Early Approach to toilet training is a method that takes time and consistent, unfaltering parental involvement. When it's done properly, it is also a method that works without adverse side-effects. As with all methods and all children, there will be occasional times of relapse, when the trained child will soil or wet his pants (see page 29 for a full discussion of regression), but even when the close parental observations, record-keeping, and prompting are concluded, most children who are toilet trained with the Early Approach continue to use their toilet skills as they progress to achieve complete voluntary toileting habits, which will include dressing and undressing, getting on and off the toilet, and washing his hands afterwards.

The Advantages of the Early Approach

- Studies show that children who begin toilet training between five and fourteen months of age manifest fewer emotional problems during the training period than those children who are toilet trained between fifteen and nineteenth months of age.

- Children who successfully complete the Early Approach to toilet training can hold back their urine and BMs and signal you when they have to use the potty. This saves their parents the cost and bother of several more years of diapering.

- A child's gastrocolonic reflex is often more predictable in infancy than it is at two or three years, giving parents a better chance of successful trips to the potty and increasing the child's motivation to avoid soiled and wet diapers.

- The early training method makes toileting a daily routine before the child is in the habit of diaper soiling, making training easier in the sense that once a child has learned to associate defecating with diaper soiling, he may resist training because it is inconvenient and a change in his routine.

- Through early training, a child comes to regard bowel movements in a diaper as unnatural and uncomfortable, so there is no struggle or resistance to using the potty for elimination.
- Some children show a preference for cleanliness at an early age, which can be used to encourage early toilet training.
- The approach can foster a stronger sense of self-esteem because it helps develop an early sense of effectiveness and competence.
- A child who is accustomed to passing BMs in the potty from an early age is likely to progress rapidly in voluntary control in the second year.

Disadvantages of the Early Approach

- The Early Approach to toilet training demands a great deal of constant parental involvement.
- Some parents may have unrealistic developmental expectations, and therefore may be disappointed when they use the Early Approach and their child does not have complete voluntary bowel and bladder control by age one.
- A highly competitive parent who wants a "superbaby" may put too much pressure on a young child, causing him to suffer emotionally throughout the training period.
- The Early Approach takes more time to complete than other methods. Studies have found that toilet training begun at five months of age will take an average of 10 months to complete, whereas training begun at twenty months of age will take 5 months to complete.[7]
- Parents must expect more periods of regressions, because a younger child is more likely to forget what he learned than an older child.

- Some babies are very irregular in passing BMs, making it difficult or impossible to catch their movements. If you can't regularly catch your child's BMs, or you repeatedly find your child in the middle of the act of defecation, the child can't be conditioned. The timing is important because the baby will not learn anything if you place him on the potty even a few seconds after he passed BMs. It's easy to become frustrated and upset with the child if you can't catch the bowel movements in time.

Do's and Don'ts of the Early Approach

DO:
- Use the Early Approach for toilet training children who are between three and fifteen months of age.
- Set realistic goals based on practical developmental expectations.
- Expect the Early Approach to condition your child through association to hold back urine and BMs and signal you when he has to use the potty.
- Prepare yourself in advance of the training period by establishing a positive and unemotional attitude, by examining your motive for choosing early training, by learning about the facts of physical development as they relate to toilet training, by obtaining the proper equipment, and by observing your child for bodily signals of elimination.
- Expect periods of regression.
- Keep track of your child's progress with the Early Approach record form on page 94.

DON'T:
- Expect a child under fifteen months to gain complete voluntary bowel and bladder control. Most children are not developmentally ready to do that at this age.

- Scold or punish your child for wetting or soiling his diaper.
- Use undue pressure to make your child follow the procedures of the Early Approach.
- Expect quick results.
- Try the Early Approach if your child is often left with baby-sitters or spends much time in day-care facilities. The process requires ongoing personal attention from one constant care-giver.

Chapter Five

The Rapid Approach

In 1974, psychologists Nathan Azrin and Richard Foxx introduced a method of toilet training for children 20 months old or older that can teach proper toileting habits in less than one day.[1] Instant potty training is the dream of many parents, but before you decide to jump right into this method, read through this chapter, which will give you a general overview of the approach and explain the advantages and disadvantages of its use. Then, if you decide the Rapid Approach is the best method of toilet training for your child get a copy of the book *Toilet Training in Less Than a Day* by Nathan A. Azrin, Ph.D. and Richard M. Foxx, Ph.D. It will give you the in-depth details you'll need to use this approach successfully.

The objective of the Rapid Approach is to teach the child mature toileting habits that he will use in an independent manner—without reminders, assistance, or continued rewards. The goal is more easily attained in one day if the parent prepares in advance by teaching the child such things as how to raise and lower his pants, how to communicate his need to use the toilet, and how to follow directions. The parents should also prepare the training area—the kitchen—by removing all distractions such as the T.V., radio, toys, and telephone.

Once training has begun, the parent will use several forms of approval and disapproval to motivate correct toileting. Positive motivators include verbal praise, snack treats, tasty fluids, and nonverbal praise like touching, hugging, kissing, and clapping. This approach also encourages proper toileting through "friends who care." Friends who care are people—friends, grandparents, teachers, siblings, television and cartoon characters, etc.—who will be happy when the child uses the toilet. Penalties for accidents (as outlined on page 121) show the parents' disapproval by making the child responsible for cleaning himself and practicing proper toileting.

The Rapid Approach program combines some basic behavioral principles into one intensive program. It uses, for example, modeling, which allows a child to imitate the actions to be learned. In this first step of the Rapid Approach, the child takes on the role of teacher and practices toilet training a wetting doll. The program encourages sensory awareness by clearly establishing the concepts of "wet" and "dry" and by creating a continuous need to urinate, which gives the child many opportunities to practice proper toileting. This approach also uses the behavioral principle of prompting, which constantly reminds the child of how the process works. Then, when the child properly uses the toilet, the parent offers immediate praise and reinforcement. The Rapid Approach to toilet training is successful when the child walks to the potty chair without a reminder and completes the entire toileting procedure without parental guidance.

Is This an Appropriate Toilet Approach for My Child?

Most children 20 months old or older can be toilet trained with the rapid method. Since all children develop at different rates, however, Azrin and Foxx suggest that parents check the child for signs of readiness that will assure he is able to follow the program. These signs include a bladder capacity that allows the child to withhold urine for several hours. A child must also show an indication of physical readiness by having enough finger- and hand-coordination to pick up objects easily, and by having the ability to walk from room to room without any

need for assistance. Finally, the child should show signs of instructional readiness: the ability to understand his parents' directions when they ask him to do such things as sit down on a chair, walk to a particular place, or imitate a simple task.

In addition to these readiness factors, other considerations influence the program's effectiveness. For example, a child with a stubborn personality may refuse to follow directions and therefore could not be trained with this approach. Also, if a child has unsuccessfully tried other methods of toilet training, the Rapid Approach may not work effectively since he may have developed a strong dislike for using the toilet. In addition, if a child is mildly mentally challenged, he cannot use the Rapid Approach unless the parent makes several changes in the method. These changes are explained in the book, *Toilet Training in Less Than a Day*. The Rapid Approach is inappropriate for a child who is severely challenged.

Even children who appear to be ready for rapid training respond differently to the Rapid Approach. The average time for complete training is about four hours. Some are trained in one hour; others may take two days, while others may not respond to this kind of training approach at all. The wide range of potential reactions to the program is evident in the comments of these parents:

"Jenny is really proud of being dry, and I'm amazed that it was so quick and easy. The entire training process took us five and a half hours."

"After an hour and fifteen minutes I gave up. I couldn't stand such total absorption in peeing in the potty."

"It was difficult at first to give up everything else and concentrate so totally on using the potty, but then I found it was nice to have an excuse to give Tommy my total and undivided attention for an extended period of time."

"I think I did everything I was supposed to do, but after eight hours of using this program, I felt like I needed a straight jacket and a bottle of tranquilizers. We quit before I got too crazy."

Look over the following lists of advantages and disadvantages. They will help you decide if you would like to try the Rapid Approach to toilet training.

The Rapid Approach is not a mysterious ritual that suddenly produces a toilet-trained child; it is a structured program that makes use of a number of factors known to enhance a child's learning ability, such as a distraction-free environment, repeated learning trials, frequent and immediate reinforcement, manual guidance, verbal instruction, and imitation. These factors are combined with the basic behavioral principles of modeling, sensory awareness, prompting, and a concrete reward and penalty system.

You know your own personality, and you know your child's abilities and temperament, and you know the basics of the Rapid Approach. Only you can decide if this is the toilet training approach that is best for you and your child. If you decide to give it a try, be sure to read the step-by-step details in the book, *Toilet Training In Less Than A Day*.

Advantages of the Rapid Approach

- A child can often be completely toilet trained in less than one day's time.
- This approach makes use of several types of learning techniques, which help children learn more quickly.
- Rapid training eliminates the frustrations of several months of traditional training.
- This method eliminates the time and money required to keep a child in diapers longer than necessary.
- Rapid training reduces the possibility of long-term parent-child conflicts over toilet-training procedures.
- Upon completion of the training period, a child is able to use the potty totally independent of grown-up supervision.

Possible Disadvantages of the Rapid Approach

- This approach to toilet training puts a great deal of pressure on the child.
- The parent must totally dedicate one day to the training procedure.
- Many parents find it difficult to maintain strict adherence to the program.
- Some parents may emphasize the penalty aspect of this approach and become too punitive.

- Parts of the procedure are subtle, and many parents may lack the self-control required for successful training.
- Some children respond to the intense training with temper tantrums and other resistant behavior.
- The approach is not likely to work for children who have had difficulty using other toilet training methods, nor for those with stubborn personalities.

Chapter Six

Teaching Good Hygiene

As soon as your child begins to release urine or bowel movements into the potty or toilet, it's time to introduce the three steps of good hygiene:

1. Wiping
2. Flushing the toilet
3. Washing hands

Wiping

Wiping is a skill that must be mastered before your child can be fully in charge of independent toileting. Although thorough and proper wiping probably won't be possible until your child is four or five, the steps of wiping should be introduced as soon as your child successfully uses the potty or toilet. As you go through each step, talk about it out loud and teach your child to follow your example:

1. Show him how many pieces of tissue are necessary (this may avoid the common dilemma of clogged toilets from children who use half a roll on each wipe).
2. Explain that it's very important for good health and cleanliness to wipe away any bowel movement (and urine for girls) that remains after going potty.
3. Show your child how to thoroughly wipe. Little

girls should learn to wipe from front to back to avoid bringing fecal matter into their vaginal opening and causing infection.
4. Always give your child a turn to practice.
5. Be sure to finish the job yourself.

Wiping usually remains a parental responsibility for quite a while after the child has achieved success with all other aspects of toileting. This is so because:

- A toddler's arms are too short to fully reach the anal area
- Toddlers lack the dexterity needed to wipe thoroughly
- The consequences of an incomplete job are annoying for child and parent alike

Once your child is physically capable of doing the job himself, hand over the responsibility. Many parents find themselves wiping bottoms long past the time their children really need help. Don't fall into this habit. Having your child take a turn after every toileting right from the start will make it easier to gradually give up the task.

Flushing

Complete independent toileting includes flushing. Right from the start help your child get into this habit. If your child is using a potty seat, "flushing" includes pouring the urine and feces from the pot into the toilet and then flushing. Your child should be in charge of that job as soon as he has the physical coordination to do it.

If your child is using a toilet seat adaptor his flushing job is, of course, easier. But he'll still need many reminders to go back and flush.

Don't be surprised if your child is afraid of flushing. The noise or the threat of being sucked down the drain has sent many a toddler running from the bathroom in tears. Others are reluctant to see their "creation" disappear. If your child is hesitant about flushing, let him leave the room and flush the toilet yourself. Most children conquer these fears in a short time and then take over the job.

Hand Washing

A 1996 study sponsored by the public health committee of the American Society for Microbiology found that hand washing has become a lost art. By watching what people do (or don't do) in public restrooms, the researchers observed that just 60 percent of those using public restrooms wash up afterward.

Hands unwashed after toileting are an extremely common means of spreading illnesses that cause diarrhea and other intestinal problems. Now is the time to instill this habit as a part of the toileting routine.

After each successful toileting, guide your child through the four steps of hand washing:

1. Wet hands
2. Soap hands
3. Rinse
4. Dry

This step will be easier to remember if you're keeping the potty in the bathroom (as recommended). It's also easier when carefully explained and guided. Don't leave your child behind with instructions to "wash your hands." Although a simple process, initially children often need help to complete this last step of toileting. Give your child a sturdy footstool and his own towel near the sink. Use a liquid soap pump dispenser; these are easier for young children to handle than a bar of soap meant for adult hands. Demonstrate each step and practice together. Young children love the feel of water and soap and so this is one part of the toilet-training process they'll enjoy. It won't be long at all before your child begs, "Let me do it myself" to show you he has mastered this important step of the toileting process.

PART II

Special Cases

Chapter Seven

Understanding Delayed Toileting

As a general rule, children start to fall into the delayed category of toilet training if they are not trained by the age of three and a half. Before you consider your child "delayed," however, remember that periods of regression in learned toileting habits are to be expected from time to time. It is not at all unusual for a child over the age of three who is completely bowel and bladder trained occasionally to find himself at the playground standing in a puddle of urine, or for this child to wake up in the morning soaking wet, or to find himself too busy to answer nature's call to defecate until it's too late and he's sitting in his own BMs. This child is experiencing common relapses, he is not delayed.

If a child without toileting difficulties is three and a half years or older, however, and his period of regression lasts for four weeks without any sign of ending, or if he has never mastered bowel and/or bladder control, then he can be considered delayed. This child could benefit from one of the toilet-training approaches explained here in Part II of this book.

Boys are more likely than girls to fall into this delayed category. The reasons for this occurrence are unclear, but in every country for which surveys have been published, the high incidence of male toilet training difficulties remains constant.

Children who are mentally challenged also are often delayed in their toilet training. In fact, several of the currently used treatments for hard-to-train normal children were first developed to train mentally challenged children and adults. Don't assume, however, that if your child is hard to train, it's because he has a low level of intelligence. Many children with normal and above normal IQs experience toilet-training difficulties.

Use the following checklist to decide whether your child might be considered delayed in his toilet training:

My child is:

Three and a half years or older and not bowel trained (does not put his BMs in the toilet on a regular basis).   _____

Three and a half years or older and not day and/or nighttime bladder trained (consistently wets his pants or diapers).   _____

Having delayed toileting problems, but not born prematurely, nor are there any other developmental problems.   _____

Experiencing a relapse in his ability to use the toilet for his bowel movements and/or urine. (This period of regression has lasted for four weeks or more.)   _____

If you can check off any of these characteristics, then the information in Part II may be just what you need to help your child learn mature toileting habits.

Why Is My Child Delayed in Using the Toilet?

There are many causes for delayed toileting. Sometimes, if you can find the reason your child is having toilet-training difficulties, it is easier to find the appropriate remedy. Following are some of the causes most commonly associated with delayed toileting.

Physical

The toilet-training approaches explained later in this chapter are not appropriate for children with physical reasons for their delay in toileting. Although only about 2 percent of children who are not toilet trained by age three have physical reasons for the delay, you should still look for the physical first.

Before you label your child as hard to train, tell your pediatrician about the toilet-training problems your child is having. Ask the doctor to check for any physical problems that could complicate the toilet-training process. He or she will be able to determine whether your child suffers from an obstruction, a milk allergy (lactose intolerance), or a urinary tract problem, or any other physical problem that can cause your child to have delayed toileting control.

Personality

It is sometimes difficult to toilet train children who have stubborn, rebellious, or negativistic personality traits. When this is the case, toilet training is only one area of child rearing that causes parent/child conflicts; rebellious children will also resist following even the simplest of directions. Statements like "Bring your shoes to me so I can put them on" can cause a screaming tantrum. When asked to pick up their toys, these children are likely to respond with, "No, I don't want to. You do it." And when asked to drink their milk, they may pretend not to hear or intentionally tip over the glass.

When a child with a resistant personality is not toilet trained by the age of three and a half, it's time to show him you mean business. You may find the approach in Chapter Nine, designed for children who are generally resistant to all toilet training, works best with this kind of child.

Stress

Some children fall into the delayed training category because they develop a persistent toileting problem in response to something stressful in their lives. It is not at all unusual for a child to experience a relapse in toilet learning when he faces situations like the birth of a sibling, the start of a new school year, moving into a new house, or a death or divorce in the family. But when the relapse becomes persistent and is unresponsive to firm reminders and traditional training methods, then this child may need a more intensive approach.

When retraining a child who is experiencing stress, it's important that you avoid being angry, punitive, or negative; this only adds to his stress load and causes further regression. It is necessary, however, to remain steadfast in your belief that wetting and/or soiling at his age (over three and a half) is not acceptable. The first step in dealing with stress-related toileting problems is to try to ease the specific stress. Also, make extra time in your day for lots of special attention, hugs, and kisses. Then establish a daily schedule that allots time for sitting on the potty every 2 hours (if possible). This will get the child back into the routine of mature toileting habits. If this doesn't stop him from soiling and/or wetting, then continue giving him the extra time and love, but move on to one of the more intensive training methods detailed in later chapters.

Parental Attitude

As difficult as it may be to accept, even the most loving and well-meaning parents can cause their children to suffer from delayed toileting. This happens when the parental attitudes that are brought to the toilet-training process are not positive, warm, or casual. Some parents begin toilet training with a highly disciplined, severe, and punitive approach. Although children can usually attain bowel and bladder control in this kind of tense mental environment, they often develop toileting problems at a later time. Other parents leave the learning of bowel and bladder control entirely up to the child. Studies have found that this lax attitude leaves children without guidance or support and can also lead to delayed toileting problems rather than to the self-mastery that parents hope for.

It is important for you to prepare yourself mentally with the appropriate calm, warm, and supportive attitude before you begin remedial training. (Attitude preparation is discussed in detail in Chapter Two.) It may be especially difficult to do this with an older child who has toileting problems, because you might feel that he knows better. But even when using remedial approaches it's imperative to refrain from using shame, ridicule, anger, threats, yelling, or excessive physical force to punish your child if he refuses to follow your directions, or if he occasionally forgets what he's supposed to do.

However, remedial approaches to toilet training do apply more pressure on the child than most of the other traditional training methods. In common with the techniques used in the Rapid Approach, some remedial approaches incorporate penalties as a logical consequence of the undesirable action. When an approach for a specific type of delayed toileting problem uses the reward and penalty system, refer to the full discussion of its use in Chapter Eight.

Remaining calm while using a system of rewards and penalties may be easier said than done for some parents. If you were unable to control your temper during your last attempt at toilet training when your child got off the potty and then immediately soiled his pants, or if you had trouble offering warmth and support when your patience was wearing thin after a series of false alarms, or if you found it repulsive to be actively involved in your child's toileting routine, then it's now time to honestly determine if you will be able to change your attitude during these remedial approaches. If you feel you can change, then reread Chapter Two to get yourself set to start again.

If you know yourself well enough to realize that you can't change your attitude, however, don't feel you must forge ahead anyway. A good parent knows when to call for help. Let someone else take over the job of remedial training—someone like your spouse, your parents, or your baby-sitter. If there is no one around who can give you a hand, and you know your personality isn't the right kind for the job, then pick up the phone and call for professional help. You might call your state or county psychological association and ask them to refer you to a psychologist in your area who has special experience with toilet-training problems. Considering the damage that a negative parental attitude can do to your child's sense of self-esteem and well-being, such a call will be well worth the effort. In only a few sessions, a psychologist can usually find the reason for the delayed toileting and suggest a remedial program that he or she will closely monitor. Then you and your child can leave toilet training behind and move on to other childhood activities.

Solving the Puzzle

Toilet training a child who is delayed in toileting skills is like putting together a jigsaw puzzle. You know what the whole picture is supposed to look like when you finish, but first you have to put each piece in its right place. First, you need to determine if your child is really "delayed." Then you must look for a possible cause of the delayed toileting. If you can pinpoint the cause, then you can toilet train in a way that is sensitive to the problem.

Your child is not a bystander in these approaches; he holds the key piece that will complete the puzzle. Before you do anything, talk to him:

- Tell him you are both going to start a new program that will help him feel comfortable using the toilet.
- If appropriate, assure him that you now have a better understanding of his problem; you aren't going to yell at him, embarrass him, hit him, or ridicule him anymore.
- Express confidence that he can follow the program and that he will attain mature toileting habits in a short time.
- Try to gain his trust in your new positive attitude, and enlist his promise of cooperation.
- Explain every detail of the program before you plan to begin. Make sure he understands *why* he's doing it, and *how* it works.

Which Program for Delayed Toileting Should My Child Use?

Children who are delayed in their toileting skills and are between the ages of three and a half and five years, can be called "mildly delayed," whereas children who have toileting problems and are over the age of five can be called "very delayed." The treatment procedures for these children are detailed in the following chapters and are divided according to the type of problem as follows:

Chapter Eight

Rewards and Penalties

Many of the remedial procedures for resolving delayed toilet training use reward and penalty systems. You already use such a system instinctively when you smile at and applaud a child's first steps and again when you withhold a privilege or send your child to his room for disobeying you. During toilet training, you can continue to use the rewards and penalties that your child is familiar with, such as the reward of staying up later at night or the penalty of the loss of TV viewing time. Since you've probably already tried the "usual" incentives and punishments in your training efforts, however, you'll find that the following procedures will help you start anew with rewards that are novel and enticing, and penalties that are logical consequences of undesirable toileting behaviors.

Rewards

Rewards are given as your child follows your directions through each step of a remedial program. This is done for two reasons: to motivate your child to want to use the toilet properly and to give positive reinforcement so he will want to continue following your directions. Although verbal praise is positive reinforcement, studies have found that physical, concrete objects are more likely to make your young child do what you want him to do. Your best bet will be to combine verbal praise with small material rewards.

The kinds of rewards you offer will depend on what your child likes. Try to select rewards that you know will motivate him; obviously, you can't motivate a child to do what you say with the promise of an oatmeal cookie if he hates oatmeal. Also, the rewards should be kept small because you may need a lot of them. You might try a combination of edible treats like candy or cookies; small toys like a water gun, plastic bracelet, or crayons; or stickers that are available in a variety of pictures and cartoon faces. (You can find a wide selection of such stickers at most card stores.)

A progress chart hung in the bathroom, displaying stars or stickers on each day that he follows your directions, may also provide incentive for your child. This can help your child achieve long-term goals and rewards. If you tell him he can have a special toy or treat when he properly uses the toilet four days in a row, he will be able to visualize those days by watching the chart.

Some parents have reported success with "surprise" rewards—small toys that can be wrapped individually in brightly colored paper and put in a large glass bowl; let your child choose one each time he deserves a reward.

Regardless of the rewards you choose, make sure that they are available to your child only when he follows the remedial toilet training procedures. Eventually, as your child learns independent toileting habits, you'll phase out the reward system, but until then, little "gifts" may give a child who is delayed in toileting skills the little incentive he needs to try harder.

Penalties

Remedial approaches to toilet training incorporate the kind of penalties that are often used by psychologists to modify a person's behavior. The following penalty system is most effectively **used** with the Rapid Approach on page 102 and the remedial approaches in Part II of this book.

Although, as mentioned earlier, you can use the following procedures along with your usual disciplinary methods, do not use any form of physical punishment such as spanking, hitting, or strapping a child to the toilet. This will not stop your child from soiling or wetting his pants; it may, in fact, aggravate the problem that is keeping your child from achieving mature toileting habits. All of the following penalties are to be used in the order given each time your child wets or soils his diaper or pants:

Penalty #1: Verbal Disapproval

When you first realize that your child has wet or soiled his pants, say a loud no to show that you're unhappy. Explain that wetting and/or soiling makes you very unhappy, and it is not what you expect from a big boy/girl. End your verbal disapproval with a positive and optimistic message such as, "I know you don't like the feel of wet and/or soiled pants, and I expect next time you'll put it in the potty/toilet." It takes only a few seconds to express your displeasure and make your point; don't drag it on to the point of nagging. (Hopefully it will also interrupt the elimination act.)

Penalty #2: Cleanliness Training

Make your child responsible for cleaning up after himself each time he wets and/or soils. After you give your verbal disapproval for wetting and/or soiling, tell your child to take off his wet pants or diaper. If he has soiled, he must wipe himself clean and rinse out the dirty pants. Then he must get dry pants and put them on. (Keep dry clothing, sponges, paper towels, and/or a mop in places where your child can get them himself.) If your child is too young to do this entirely by himself, help him only by physically guiding his movements. Help his hands pull down the wet pants and wipe himself, then guide his legs into the proper pant legs, and then assist his hands as he pulls them up. Have your child put the wet pants into the hamper or laundry bag.

If the wetting and/or soiling incident left a puddle or pile on the floor, make your child clean it up. If his efforts don't satisfy your standards, finish the job later when he can't see you.

Penalty #3: Toileting Practice

When your child and the floor are clean, it's time to practice what he should have done when he first felt the urge to urinate and/or defecate.

Go to the place where the wetting and/or soiling occurred. Tell your child he must practice moving quickly from that spot to the toilet. Once in the bathroom, he must take down his pants, and then get onto the potty or toilet seat. Then he must get off the seat and pull up his pants. Repeat this routine 10 times after every wetting and/or soiling incident. This task will be easier to do if your child wears clothing that is easy to get off and on; overalls, long dresses, or pants with buttons or snaps make proper toileting more difficult than it needs to be.

As your child is practicing this toileting routine, talk to him. Explain *why* he must do this and then tell him what it will accomplish: "You wet yourself. This practice will help you remember what to do the next time you need to pass urine or BMs." Emphasize the need for speed: "You must hurry so you will be on the toilet/potty before the urine or BMs come out."

At first, some children enjoy the "game" of running to the bathroom, but soon get bored and protest when you insist they must practice after each wetting and/or soiling incident. If your child does not want to practice toileting, don't skip over it. Penalties are not supposed to be enjoyable. Guide him through the steps manually, but always remember to stay relaxed and unemotional as you help him get to the bathroom, make his hands pull down his pants, and guide him onto the seat.

Penalty #4: Sensory Awareness Training

The goal of this part of the penalty procedure is to develop a child's understanding of the difference between wet and dry.

After your child has finished his toileting practice, bring him to the place where he put his wet pants. Have him touch the wet pants and say, "wet." Then have him touch the crotch of his dry pants and say, "dry." Do this

10 times over the 2-hour period following each wetting/ soiling incident (approximately every 12 minutes).

If your child objects to this procedure, again guide his body to the place where the wet pants are, and then place his hands on the wet pants and on the dry pants. In a calm voice *you* say "wet" and "dry."

General Tips

Here are some tips to help you manage the entire reward and penalty system:

- Rewards should be offered within 2 seconds of a successful act, and the penalty sequence should also be administered the very moment you realize that your child has wet and/or soiled his pants.
- The reward and penalty system requires immediate feedback, as well as constant supervision, so it is very important that you use a remedial approach only when you have time to be at home with your child.
- Before you begin a remedial approach, talk with your child about the rewards and penalties that you will be using. Let him know what is expected of him, what will happen when he follows your directions, and what will happen when he does not.
- Give out rewards and penalties in a calm and casual manner. Toileting should be viewed as a natural human process, not something that is cause for joyous and boisterous celebration. At the same time, failure to follow your toileting directions should not be cause for violent outbursts of anger. If your child believes that his toileting habits are the most important thing in the world to you, he may soon learn how to use proper and improper toileting to manipulate your actions.

Chapter Nine

Toilet Training the Generally Resistant Child of Three and a Half to Five

If your child is between the ages of three and a half and five years old and will not use the potty or toilet for passing urine or BMs during the day or night, he may be called "generally resistant to toilet training." When this is the case, stop whatever method of toilet training you're using, and start toilet training all over again from step one. The remedial method in this chapter will help you make a fresh start by tightening up the training procedure and establishing an organized system of toileting.

Preparation

Attitude

Many children who are generally resistant to toilet training regard toileting as the one aspect of their lives over which they have total control. It is the only thing that gives them leverage with their parents because they know proper toileting makes their parents happy, and improper toileting makes them angry and frustrated. This is a form of power that a rebellious or negativistic child may be reluctant to give up.

Before taking another step in your toilet training, re-read the information on "attitude" in Chapter Two. The most difficult part of training a child who is delayed in his toileting because he is basically stubborn, is maintaining a calm attitude. The information in that chapter will help you to stay strong mentally.

An additional difficulty in training a delayed child is caused by the thin line parents walk between being patient and being insistent. This sense of confusion was expressed in a letter I recently received from a mother whose four-year-old son refused to use the toilet. She wrote:

"We have always been uncertain as to how firm to be about toilet training. Frankly, we don't know in which direction to proceed. We have been fumbling around trying just about everything, but yet not following through on anything. We are confused on how to deal with all the emotions that may be involved, like embarrassment, stubbornness, and lack of confidence. Can you help us get back on the right track to salvage whatever is left of our son's self-esteem?"

This mother needed to resolve her ambivalent feelings about toilet training before she could take charge and help her son. She needed to confront her son and tell him that it was time he used the toilet. She had to be firm and persistent without feeling guilty about the confrontation. Without yelling or hitting, she had to make him understand that nothing else was acceptable.

As you start your new program of toilet training, make it very clear to your child that proper toileting is what you expect because it's part of being a grown-up person, nothing more, nothing less. Proper toileting will not make you deliriously happy, just as improper toileting will not make you furious. Rewards and penalties will be given calmly and without annoyance.

Although you can expect your child to be totally opposed to your new attitude, don't let that make you less determined. As proper toileting attempts become part of his daily routine, and he begins to experience some success, he will gradually become less resistant.

Relationship

Very often delayed toileting puts pressure on the parent/child relationship. You may find that the bonds you worked so diligently to secure are cracking under the weight of anger, disappointment, argument, and frustration. Ironically, at the same time that delayed toileting problems are pulling you apart from your child, your child is depending on your love and support to help him through this difficult time.

Before you begin the retraining period, take time to rebuild your relationship with your child. In a warm and nurturing environment, most children are eager to please their parents by doing what they ask. This desire to conform eliminates the parents' need to threaten, bribe, or demand.

If, when you begin training your resistant child, you find yourself too upset or angry to remain warm and nurturing, then stop all training efforts until you feel calm again. Or you can find someone else to take over the training process, or seek professional help.

Sensory Awareness

Children who resist using the potty or toilet may be confused about what exactly happens during the elimination process. In the safety of their diapers or training pants, they can eliminate in a passive manner without any realization of the true effect, or any responsibility for taking care of themselves.

To improve your child's sensory awareness of the elimination process, it is often helpful to take off his clothes and let him run naked. Obviously this is easier to do outside in warm weather or on a hard washable floor. Being naked will help your child understand what occurs during elimination; it will relieve fears he may have about what will happen to him if he relieves himself without the security of his diapers or pants, and it may motivate him to hold his urine and BMs until he is on the potty or toilet.

One mother found that her son, who liked to hide in the closet to eliminate, became very upset and frustrated when she took away his diaper. "He acted like you or I would act if someone took away our toilet when we really had to go," she said. "He seemed desperate to find a special place to go, but unfortunately, that place still wasn't going to be the toilet. So I put down newspapers in the corner of the bathroom and told him if he wanted a special, private place, he could go there. It worked better than I had hoped. He used the newspaper two times and then the next time I asked him if he would like to try the potty, he said 'Yes' for the first time in his life!''

Treatment

Routine

When training a child who resists all aspects of toileting, it's best to concentrate on one skill at a time, so begin the remedial training with emphasis on bowel control.

Establish a daily toileting routine that is structured and consistent. Without fail, have your child sit on the potty or toilet 15 minutes after he finishes his breakfast, since the gastrocolonic reflex makes this the most likely time for a bowel movement. Try to keep him sitting on the bowl for at least 5 minutes. If he does not defecate, let him get off for 10 minutes; then put him back on for another 5 minutes. Do this again after lunch and dinner. If your child wants to sit on the potty or toilet at other times of the day, let him. Or, if you see bodily signs like grunting or face reddening at other times of the day, take him to the toilet. But be sure to insist on at least three sittings each day.

In the beginning, stay with your child in the bathroom to encourage him. Repeatedly remind him why he's sitting on the toilet. (This is not a time to play with toys.) Once your child is used to the routine, you can then phase yourself out of his toileting time. Leave the bathroom for a few seconds, and gradually increase the time you stay away until he is totally responsible for getting on, staying on, and getting off the toilet by himself.

A regular toileting regime may seem more acceptable to your child if other aspects of his day, such as sleeping, eating, and exercising, are also scheduled into a daily routine. As you begin this remedial approach to toilet training, take time to organize and implement a consistent daily schedule.

Progress Chart

	SUNDAY	MONDAY	TUESDAY	WEDNESDAY	THURSDAY	FRIDAY	SATURDAY
Potty Times:							
BM Time: ___ pants ___ potty ___							
Potty Times:							
BM Time: ___ pants ___ potty ___							
Potty Times:							
BM Time: ___ pants ___ potty ___							
Potty Times:							
BM Time: ___ pants ___ potty ___							
Potty Times:							
BM Time: ___ pants ___ potty ___							

Record Keeping

Use the chart on page 129 to keep a written record of the training process. This chart will show even the slightest improvement in toilet habits that you might otherwise overlook It may also show you a pattern of defecation that will help you know the best time to put your child on the toilet. You can use the chart to motivate your child to use the toilet if he can help you record the times of toileting and can paste a star on the days he puts his BMs in the toilet.

Keep the chart in the bathroom and use it. Accurate written records will help you stick to the kind of consistent toileting routine that your child needs to help him overcome his resistance to proper toileting.

Rewards and Penalties

Most children who stubbornly resist all toilet training efforts need to be motivated even before they will begin to cooperate. If the previously mentioned strategies don't motivate your child to practice proper toileting skills, use the reward and penalty system explained in Chapter Eight. This program of incentives and punishments, if used properly and consistently, will motivate your child to urinate and defecate in the proper place. When you first begin the training program, keep your child in diapers. (See Appendix A for the manufacturers of large-size diapers.) It is too messy and too discouraging to use training pants when you know your child won't use the toilet. As soon as you see some signs of successful toileting, switch to training pants. These may further motivate your child to practice "grown-up" toileting habits. If he wets or soils the pants, calmly change them and assure him that you know he'll soon be using the toilet.

Once your child is comfortable with passing his BMs into the toilet, he will probably start using the toilet for urinating without any further training. If he does not, then continue your BM training routine, but bring your child to the bathroom to urinate every 2 hours throughout the day. Sometimes, he will go; sometimes, he will not. But the routine will eventually get him in the habit of using the toilet for all his toileting needs.

Chapter Ten

Helping Children with Delayed Bowel Control

How to Help Children Three and a Half to Five Years Old Gain Daytime Bowel Control

By the time children are three and a half years old, bowel "control" is usually not the problem. Unless there is a physical or developmental problem, most children at this age have the physical ability to control their bowel sphincter muscle. They now recognize the sensation of a full rectum that needs to be emptied, and they can hold back the stools and release them at will. The real problem with mildly delayed bowel control is *where* the child chooses to exercise that control.

When some children feel the urge to defecate, they hold back their BMs until they can get to a special spot they have picked out for this purpose—usually a spot that is private, such as a corner of a room or a closet. Joey, for example, liked to sneak off to the garage. "The first few times I found piles of poop in the garage," said his mom, "I thought a dog was getting in at night. But then one day I walked in and found Joey standing in the corner and grunting. He looked so startled when he saw me; this was obviously something he wanted to do in private. I couldn't understand, since he knew when he had to go, why he didn't use the toilet like he did when he had to urinate?"

The fact that Joey was standing when his mom found him passing BMs may explain why he felt more comfortable in the garage than on the toilet. Some children become accustomed to defecating in a standing or lying position, and can't easily adjust to sitting.

Other children with bowel training problems will pass BMs only when they have a diaper on. Many of these children wear underpants all day; many go to school or day care and appear to be completely trained. They hold back their bowel movement until nighttime when they can wear a diaper. As soon as the diaper is on, they are able to relax the rectal sphincter muscle and pass BMs.

Some children who won't put their BMs in the toilet or potty, ignore the need to defecate until they can be alone in their private place or until their diaper is on. Others who know they will be scolded when they don't put their BMs in the toilet, hold back for as long as they possibly can. Unfortunately, all this holding back often leads to chronic constipation. When the stools remain too long in the colon, the body draws out too much water from them, and they become very hard and difficult to pass. When the rectum becomes impacted in this way, its water-absorbing capacity becomes impaired and watery stools may leak out even though the child is constipated. Now the child who initially didn't want to sit on the toilet or potty to pass BMs has the additional aggravation and discomfort of painful elimination, as well as the embarrassment of soiled pants.

One mom, for example, was having trouble bowel training her four-year-old daughter because she didn't realize how difficult it was for her to pass BMs. "I knew that her stools were quite often hard and large," she said, "but I didn't realize how much it hurt Jenny to pass them."

If your child is caught in this cycle of withholding BMs and suffering from constipation, talk to your pediatrician before beginning any of the following remedial approaches. He or she may prescribe a stool softener, a laxative, or an enema to relieve the pain of elimination. The doctor may also recommend a diet that is high in fibrous foods such as fruits, vegetables, and bran; and low in binding substances such as junk foods, and dairy products like milk, cheese, chocolate, and peanut butter.

*Some children resist using the bathroom, preferring
more creative private spots.*

Constipation may also be relieved through a program of
regular exercise and daily toileting that allows time to
sit on the bowl and relax.

Before you begin training a child who is mildly delayed in his bowel control, consider the possible reasons
why your child is withholding his BMs. As explained
previously, reasons for toileting delay problems may in-

clude stress factors, personality factors, and parental attitudes. In addition to these factors, bowel delay is often
caused by emotional fears connected to the toilet training process itself. For some children, the sensation of
letting go of BMs for a free-fall into the open space of
a bowl, for example, is a never-before-experienced act
that they may avoid because it's unfamiliar territory.
Other children are possessive of their BMs because they
feel it's a part of themselves that they don't want to lose.

Some children are afraid of the toilet bowl itself. They
imagine falling into the bowl and being swallowed up,
or they're afraid that since a part of themselves (their
urine and BMs) fall down and get flushed away, so might
their penis or buttocks do the same. Some (especially
those with older siblings or friends who may tell scary
stories) are afraid that a monster or alligator will come
up out of the bowl and bite or grab them.

Many children are afraid of the flushing sound of the
toilet. Others don't like the feel of the cold seat on their
buttocks. Some children avoid using the potty or toilet
because they associate it with something fearful or painful. If, for example, the child once lost his balance and
fell into the bowl, or scraped himself on the urine deflector, or felt pain when passing a hardened stool, he
may feel that his diaper or the floor is a safer place
to eliminate.

Very often parents are unaware of their child's emotional fears because it's difficult for children to verbalize
these kinds of inner conflicts. If your child is having trouble learning bowel control, take some time to encourage
him to discuss his feelings about using the toilet. If he
does admit a fear, don't laugh because it's a silly notion,
or brush it off with a brisk "That's nonsense." Adults
who admit their fears to the people who love them don't
expect to be laughed at, or brushed off, or yelled at,
or punished—neither should children. Take your child's
worries seriously. Then with patience and sensitivity,
work to convince him that no harm will come to him
when he uses the toilet.

How you do this depends largely on the particular fear
your child is experiencing, but in general, your goal is
to slowly bring your child to view the potty or toilet as
a neutral and necessary part of your household that can-

not hurt him. Parents have done this in a number of sensitive and yet imaginative ways. You might want to try the following suggestions, or you can work with your child to discover your own.

"Billy wouldn't put his BMs into the potty. I knew he had the control to hold back and he knew when he had to go because he would sneak off to the garage to pass them, but I couldn't get him to go while he was urinating on the potty. I thought maybe he was afraid of how it would feel, so one day I gave him an enema. (He didn't object to that because he often had his temperature taken rectally.) Then I sat him on the potty. Naturally, he wasn't able to hold back the bowel movement, and for the first time, he passed his BMs into the potty. Ever since then, he's had very little trouble using the potty for both his urine and BMs."

"Karen would not let me toilet train her because she was afraid of falling into the toilet and being flushed away. No matter how many times I told her this wouldn't happen and promised not to flush until she was off, she still insisted she was afraid. Finally, I took a large doll (one to which she had no particular attachment) and dropped it into the toilet. Karen seemed delighted to see that the doll did not (and could not) fall through the hole at the bottom of the bowl. She also realized that the toilet did not automatically flush as soon as something fell into it. Next we put the doll on the toilet adapter seat and held here tightly so she wouldn't fall in. Then I sat on the toilet so Karen could see that I was safe from harm. Finally, it was Karen's turn to sit on the toilet adapter seat. With only a bit of hesitation, Karen proudly lifted herself right up onto the seat. Her fear was gone."

"Sean was bladder and bowel trained on a toilet adapter seat when he was twenty months old. Then, just before his fourth birthday, he refused to sit on the toilet. Urinating was no problem because he stood up "like Daddy," but he was soiling his pants and suffering from constipation. Apparently, someone at nursery school told him that alligators live in toilets, and he was not going to risk getting bitten by an alligator. He refused to use a "baby" potty chair, and although he was embarrassed by his soiling, he wouldn't believe me that there were no alligators in the toilet.

"One night I decided it was time for Sean to learn all about toilets. I took off the tank lid and showed him how the water enters the bowl when it's flushed. Then we went down to the cellar to see the pipes that lead out to the street sewers. Knowing how a toilet works, and seeing how small the pipes are (certainly too small for alligators), seemed to help Sean face his fears. Then I suggested that he watch me sit on the toilet with my clothes on. We both remained safe and unharmed. This process only took one evening, and yet it worked. Although Sean still checks out the bowl before he sits down, he's 'cured' of his fear of alligators in the bowl."

"One day Missy and I were in a public restroom and I flushed the toilet while she was still standing next to the bowl and pulling up her pants. The flush was so loud and powerful that it scared her and she cried for the next half hour. After that she refused to use any toilet except the one in our house. This wasn't much more than an inconvenience until we went away on vacation. Missy began to wet and soil her pants because she refused to use the toilet in the hotel room.

"After two days of accidents and crying, I decided it was time to do something specific about her fear of flushing. First, I invited her to watch me sit on the toilet so she could see that I could go to the bathroom without worrying that the toilet would flush by itself. Then I told her to stand out in the hall while I flushed so she could hear the sound it made without getting scared by being too close. Later, I invited her to stand in the doorway while I flushed again, then later she stood inside the doorway. Little by little, Missy came up close to the toilet and finally flushed it herself. That night, without any prompting from me, Missy walked into the bathroom, sat on the toilet, had a bowel movement, and flushed. Now I feel badly that I didn't pay attention to her fear much sooner. I thought she would get over it by herself eventually, and although I'm sure she would have, with my help we could have avoided a lot of embarrassment and worry in the meantime."

These mothers discovered the emotional fear that was keeping their children from attaining bowel control and then found a way to ease the fear. If you cannot find the reason, or if you have no success in overcoming your child's resistance to using the potty or toilet, the following remedial approaches may help him to learn to put his BMs in the proper place.

Treatment

Approach #1: Directive Training

1. Plan to spend the next few weeks at home with your child so that you will constantly be available to bring him to the bathroom, to clean up his inevitable messes, and to watch for telltale signs of the need to defecate, such as sneaking off to be alone, grunting, face reddening, or quieting.
2. Establish a daily routine of potty sitting. If you know the time of day that your child is likely to defecate, you can use that knowledge to time your trips to the potty or toilet. It is probably better, however, to create a regular schedule of potty sitting after meals and naps (or every 2 hours if possible) because an older child may resist your efforts to train him by holding back his bowel movements during the time he usually defecates. Have your child sit on the potty for 5 minutes. If he doesn't pass his BMs, allow him to leave the room for 5 minutes, and then bring him back to the potty for another 5-minute try. Do this on a regular schedule throughout the day.
3. Watch for signs of constipation. If you notice that your child is not moving his bowels at all during the training period, contact your pediatrician. Ask him or her to suggest a stool softener, laxative, or enema.
4. Your child may try to hide from you and defecate in private. That's why you'll need to stay near him

throughout the training period, and guide (or carry) him to the bathroom when you think he has to go.

5. To motivate him to follow your directions, use the reward and penalty system outlined in Chapter Eight.

A few weeks of consistent, scheduled potty sitting, followed up with rewards and penalties, may be all you'll need to help your child learn to put his BMs in the potty or toilet.

Approach #2: Step-by-Step Desensitization

The goal of this training approach is to bring your child, slowly and over a period of several days or even weeks, to sit on the toilet or potty and pass his BMs without fear. This is the same kind of desensitizing objective that is sometimes used with people who are afraid of traveling in airplanes. First the fearful person talks about what he wants to do; then he imagines himself doing it. Then he holds a toy airplane and imagines himself riding in it without fear; then he visits an airport. Then he gets on a plane just for a quick look around; then he enters the plane, sits down, and then leaves. Next he takes a short trip; then a longer one, and so on until the goal is accomplished and the fear is gone.

Desensitizing for bowel control works in a similar way except it includes a penalty and reward system for motivation. The program is as follows:

Step One

Talk with your child about this method of toilet training. During your discussion, be sure to:

- Tell him you're going to help him learn to use the potty (or toilet) for passing BMs just like Grandma, Grandpa, and big brother always do.
- Ask him to talk about his views, feelings, and worries related to toilet training.
- Express confidence that he can do it.
- Assure him of your support and love.

Step Two
He must agree to the following rule:
BMs MUST BE PASSED IN THE BATHROOM
It is perfectly acceptable if your child goes into the bathroom and defecates in his diaper, or in his pants, or on the floor, or in the tub, or standing in the corner, or in any other way that he wants—as long as he's in the bathroom.

Step Three
Explain to your child, and then incorporate, the system of rewards and penalties outlined in Chapter Eight.

Step Four
Once your child is in the habit of defecating in the bathroom, phase out the rewards and penalties for this action. Now tell him he must sit on the potty or toilet when he feels the urge to pass his BMs. Assure him that he can keep his diaper or pants on, but he must be sitting on the seat.

Calmly remind him of the penalty system that will be used if he refuses, and then show him the new reward incentives you have for him when he complies.

Step Five
When your child regularly sits on the toilet or potty and passes his BMs with his diaper or pants on, phase out the rewards for this action. Now tell him that when he sits on the potty or toilet you are going to undo the tabs or pins on his diaper (although he will still wear the diaper), or if he wears underpants, you will lower the pants to a point just below his navel.

Again, review the penalty system that will be used, and display the rewards that will be offered.

Most children don't find this part of Step Five objectionable. Once your child gets used to opened diapers or lowered pants, you can move toward the goal of completely removing the diapers or pants by revealing just a bit more flesh each time he sits on the bowl. Pull the diaper or pants just a bit further off the buttocks each time. If you can do this without your child noticing— fine. But if he notices what you're doing and complains about it, firmly but casually explain what you're doing and reactivate the reward and penalty system.

Step Six

Once you have the diaper or pants completely off your child, he might stop passing his BMs on the potty or toilet. If that happens, go back to Step One and start over again.

If your child does pass his BMs into the potty or toilet without his diaper or pants on, continue to reward him each time until he no longer needs your guidance or prompting to go into the bathroom, take down his pants, get on the toilet or potty, and pass his BMs. This kind of self-initiated toileting is the goal of all toilet-training programs. Once it is accomplished, your child is trained.

Approach #3: The Rapid Approach

The Rapid Approach explained in Chapter Five is sometimes used with successful results to toilet train children with bowel training problems.

How to Help Children Who Are Mildly Delayed in Nighttime Bowel Control

Nighttime bowel control is generally attained between the ages of one and two without any training efforts. However, if your child is soiling himself while asleep:

- He probably doesn't need a remedial training approach; he needs a checkup by his pediatrician. There may be a physical reason that the anal sphincter muscle is relaxing during sleep.
- It is most important to establish a daily toileting routine for your child that will ensure plenty of time each day to sit on the potty or toilet. It's not unusual for a child's day to end without leaving time for leisurely toileting; this may lead to consti-

pation, which in its chronic stages causes stools to leak out—even during the night.
- In addition to the daily toileting routine, allow time for sitting on the toilet or potty each night before bedtime.
- Don't use the reward and penalty system to deal with this problem unless your child suffers from chronic constipation and needs motivation to sit on the toilet to pass BMs.

How to Help Children Over the Age of Five Gain Daytime Bowel Control

Children who are five years old or older and repeatedly and involuntarily pass BMs in their pants (or places other than the toilet or potty), have a condition called *encopresis*. Some children who have this problem have never attained mature bowel control habits (primary encopresis), whereas others have regressed to soiling after having successfully attained a period of bowel control (secondary encopresis).

Whether the child's soiling is a primary or secondary condition, the characteristics are usually the same:

- Children with encopresis soil once to several times each day.
- Children often wait until after school when they are at home to soil.
- Most often encopresis is not caused by an emotional disturbance, but rather is an inherited tendency toward constipation.
- Many children who won't use the toilet hold back their BMs so they won't soil their pants. This causes chronic constipation.
- Children who have had painful bowel movements while they were constipated tend to hold back their BMs to avoid repeating the painful experience. This results in a vicious cycle because the longer they

hold back, the harder and therefore more difficult their stools are to pass.

- Children who suffer severe constipation may lose the urge to defecate because their colon becomes distended with feces.
- Watery stools seep past the hardened stools of a constipated child. His pants will then be soiled even though he made no conscious effort to defecate.

Parental Attitude

Most parents are unprepared for the problem of encopresis. You are reacting like many other parents if you get angry when it happens. It's hard not to be upset by something that is smelly, messy, and socially unacceptable. As unacceptable as soiling may be, however, the problem affects large numbers of children (1.5 percent of the seven- and eight-year-olds in the Western world), and for reasons that aren't fully understood, it affects boys three and a half times more often than girls.

If your child suffers from persistent soiling, you can help him overcome the problem, but first you have to get rid of your anger. In the vast majority of cases, the condition is not the child's fault. Even if your child seems unconcerned by his soiling and you believe he's doing it as a deliberate act of defiance, most often the soiling is caused by involuntary leakage of feces past the sphincter muscle. That's why you can't do anything to help the situation by screaming, "You're too old for this. Cut it out!"

Although remedies such as severe beatings, harsh punishments, and acts of cruelty like branding the buttocks and smearing the body with feces have been used over the years to stop childhood soiling, they have proven to be ineffective in controlling the problem. Only within the past 15 to 20 years have effective treatments for encopresis been developed, and with each treatment the probability of success depends largely on a parental attitude that is patient, supportive, and encouraging. So, although it may be difficult to remain calm while toilet training an older child who refuses to use the toilet for passing BMs, it is an essential element of the treatment program.

Mothers throughout the country have written to me about the problem of encopresis. Their letters show how difficult it is to manage the conflicting emotions of sympathy and love with the anger and frustration:

"I'm at my wits' end. My son will hold his bowel movement for days and then will finally go in his pants. My pediatrician says to wait for him to outgrow it, but every time it happens I lose my temper and we have terrible fights. I don't know what to do anymore."

"My son will not do BMs in the potty. My doctor says this is normal for a boy, and I should try to stay calm. Other mothers have told me the same thing, but these people don't know what it's like to live with this problem!"

"My daughter refuses to have BMs in the toilet. I discussed this with her doctor and got no satisfaction. I know what the problem is; I just don't know what to do about it."

"I have been told that encopresis is not an uncommon problem. The fact that other children act similarly does not make it any less distressing to me. My son can give me absolutely no reason why he doesn't use the toilet for his BMs. No matter how much I punish him, he still messes his pants. It's driving me crazy."

"My child still has bowel movements in his pants. I am trying not to push him too hard about this, but I'm getting very frustrated because I don't see him getting any better. I think it might be time to start showing him how angry it makes me."

It will be easier for these mothers and for you to maintain a positive attitude while you help your child gain mature bowel habits if you keep in mind that bowel control involves training the anal sphincter muscle to perform in an appropriate manner and at an appropriate time. Remember, too, that *all* muscle training programs take time and patience. If you enrolled your child in a youth bodybuilding program, you would instinctively know that screaming, threatening, ridiculing, or beating would not encourage him to continue training to reach his goal. He would quickly lose interest in the program and avoid the gym at all cost. So it is with bowel training; an angry, harsh trainer will drive the child away from the bathroom.

Treatment

The first step in treating a child who continually soils his pants is to find out if there is a physical reason for the soiling. Explain the situation to your pediatrician and ask him or her to examine your child for organic problems. The most common physical reasons for soiling are:

- *Neurogenic megacolon* (Hirschsprung's disease), which is characterized by the absence of normal ganglion cells in the colonic muscles whose contractions and dilations move feces into the rectum. This condition must be corrected surgically.
- *Anatomic megacolon,* which is caused by obstructing lesions and tumors in the bowel.

If your pediatrician finds a physical reason for your child's soiling, the treatment program in this book should not be used to stop the problem. Your pediatrician will explain what medical intervention is necessary.

If, however, your pediatrician finds that there is no physical reason for the soiling, as is most often the case, then it's time to start a toilet-training routine that will help your child gain complete voluntary control of his bowel.

Once parents find that there is no physical reason for their child's soiling, their first question is usually "Why does he do this?" This question is difficult to answer because most likely the condition is caused by many things. In some cases there is a relationship between encopresis and factors such as too strict or too lax toilet training, harsh and punitive parental attitudes toward toilet training, stress, and the child's own personality.

The most common cause of encopresis by far, however, is severe and chronic constipation. Constipation can cripple a child's ability to control his bowel movements. As with younger children who have bowel-training problems, when a child withholds his stools (whether because he's stubborn and doesn't want to use the toilet, or he's afraid of the toilet, or he's too busy playing, or he's under stress, or he was born with a predisposition to constipation, or whatever the reason) the colon expands to hold on to the feces; the body continues drawing water from them, and they become hard, dry, and difficult to pass. Each time the child withholds the stools, the colon becomes further impacted. The child begins to lose the sensation that signals the need to defecate. The muscles lose their ability to push feces along to the rectum, and although constipation is evident, watery stools leak past the impacted feces, and soil the child's pants. Although most people (70 percent) have a bowel movement each day, the absence of a movement does not necessarily indicate constipation. Your child may move his bowel a little every day and still be constipated, or he may go only every three days and yet not be constipated. No matter how often or how infrequently your child defecates, you can assume he is constipated if his stools are hard and difficult to pass. Occasionally blood may be present in the stool, because hard stools can cause a small tear in the anus.

Obviously, the way to stop the soiling is to stop the constipation, but constipation often causes a vicious cycle of bowel problems that is not so easily handled. Even when the stools become soft, and the muscles in the colon regain their strength, and the child once again feels the urge to defecate, he may still hold back his stools because he's afraid of the pain he has learned to associate with defecation. Because he still holds back, he once again becomes constipated. Therefore, a treatment program for encopresis will most often include treatment for constipation as well as the establishment of long-term eating and toileting habits that will prevent constipation, and therefore stool withholding, in the future.

The problem of encopresis does seem to improve over time, so a number of children are "cured" without any kind of treatment program. Although it's comforting to know that children can outgrow this problem by themselves, most experts in the field of child development recommend some kind of intervention. This is because during the time that a child is waiting for the condition to pass, he suffers tremendous emotional pain from the constant shame, ridicule, isolation, and parental disapproval he experiences each day. If the condition advances to severe constipation, he may also suffer from physical symptoms such as abdominal pain, stomach distension, headaches, dizziness, and nausea. All of this mental and physical pain seems so unnecessary when, with proper treatment, the situation usually improves in two to three weeks and disappears in two to three months.

Approach #1: Habit Training

The following program, adapted from one developed by the psychologist Logan Wright,[1] is practical, direct, and economical. It will be effective if the routine is strictly followed, with a firm commitment to seeing it through to success. The procedure is as follows:

Step One: Regular Toileting

- Your child must sit on the toilet and try to defecate every morning as soon as he wakes (or at another time of day that is consistently more convenient).
- If he cannot produce at least one-quarter to one-half cup of feces on his own, give him a glycerine suppository (these are available at drugstores without a prescription), and then make sure he eats breakfast.
- Right after breakfast, lead him back to the toilet because he will probably need to defecate.
- If he still cannot (or will not) pass BMs into the toilet, give him an enema as soon as he gets off the toilet. Children's Fleet enemas are available at drugstores without a prescription. These enemas are premixed, easy to use, and disposable. You should use 1 ounce of enema solution for every 20 pounds of body weight. If your child's bowel is severely impacted, he may even need a second enema when you first begin the program (but never use more than two enemas in one day). If this is the case, fill the enema container with lukewarm tap water and administer it again after 1 hour. If you

are opposed to giving your child an enema on a daily basis, you can give it every other day, or use Approach #2, which follows on page 149.

To conquer encopresis a daily bowel movement at a specific time is necessary. This allows the child's colon to regain its normal shape, muscle tone, and functioning; it also prevents daily soiling.

Step Two: Independent Toileting

After you have established daily bowel movements for two weeks and there are no more signs of soiling, it's time to begin weaning your child from suppositories and enemas.

- Choose one day of the week and eliminate all suppositories and enemas for the day.
- For the following day and the rest of the week, continue using the external aids if your child does not defecate on his own during the first toilet sitting.
- If at the end of one week's time there has been no sign of soiling, eliminate another day of external aids, and so on until the use of enemas and suppositories is completely eliminated.
- If soiling occurs during the weaning process, add back one day's use of suppositories for every soiling incident until, if necessary, you are back to using suppositories every day.
- Begin the weaning process again after the child goes one week without soiling.

The program is over when the child goes two weeks without soiling after all external aids are discontinued.

Step Three: Record Keeping

Strict adherence to a regular toileting procedure is crucial to the success of this program, and phasing out external aids depends on an exact record of soiling incidents over a certain period of time. Since the average length of this program is 15 to 20 weeks (a long time to hold this much information in your head), it will be most helpful to keep written records.

Use the Progress Charts on page 150 to follow your child's progress. The sample chart on page 155 will help you see how the information is to be recorded.

Follow this procedure for keeping your chart.

- Make several copies of the chart on page 150 to give you forms to use each month.
- Check off each toileting procedure as it is completed.
- Note if there are any signs of soiling and at what time of the day; this may show you a soiling pattern, and therefore a better time for sitting on the toilet.
- Note the days you don't use external aids in the toileting routine.
- When your child goes two weeks without using suppositories and without soiling, the remedial program is over.

Step Four: Rewards and Penalties

A daily toileting routine and the use of enemas and suppositories will help your child gain regularity in his bowel movements. Although this is one goal of the program, the ultimate goal is to motivate your child to want to pass daily bowel movements in the toilet without the use of external aids and to take the initiative to allow time each day for sitting on the toilet.

The reward and penalty system will help you motivate your child's desire to reach these goals. It will give positive reinforcement to his successful toileting attempts and uses penalties that are a logical consequence of the undesirable act of soiling.

Rewards and penalties should be given as follows:

- Examine your child's clothing every hour for cleanliness. If your child has not soiled, give him a reward according to the directions on page 120.
- If he has soiled, administer the penalty procedure explained on page 121.

Step Five: Constipation Control

When you begin this treatment program, your child's soiling problem should gradually disappear with the daily use of suppositories and enemas. However, your child's attempts to maintain the routine of daily defecation without these external aids will be sabotaged if he again starts to hold back BMs because of painful elimination. That's why long-term constipation control is an important aspect of the total program.

You can help your child prevent the problem of recurring constipation by following these guidelines:

• If you notice your child's stools are starting to become large and hard, ask your pediatrician to recommend a natural-fiber stool softener that can be taken as part of an ongoing maintenance program.
• Change your child's diet to include more fiber through whole-grain breads and bran cereals, fruit such as peaches and pears (leave the skins on), and vegetables such as peas, beans, cauliflower, and broccoli. You will also find natural laxatives like prunes, prune juice, raisins, and lots of water and juices to be especially helpful. Restrict your child's intake of binding foods: sweets, white flour products, chocolate, and dairy products. Milk should be limited to 1 pint a day
• Be sure your child gets plenty of physical exercise. A day of passive TV or video watching makes it more difficult for the digestive system to do its job properly.

Approach #2: Constipation Control

This approach is a standard pediatric practice for treating persistent soiling that occurs because of chronic constipation.[2] This approach is different than Approach #1 because it does not require a daily enema. Although this method takes a month or so longer to complete than Habit Training, it is a practical answer to the problem for parents who are opposed to daily enemas. The procedure that follows should be supervised by your pediatrician:

Encopresis Progress Chart

Week #___	SUNDAY	MONDAY	TUESDAY	WEDNESDAY	THURSDAY	FRIDAY	SATURDAY
sit on toilet							
suppository							
breakfast							
enema							
sit on toilet							
BM in toilet							
soiling							
Week #___							
sit on toilet							
suppository							
breakfast							
enema							
sit on toilet							
BM in toilet							
soiling							

Encopresis Progress Chart

Week #___	SUNDAY	MONDAY	TUESDAY	WEDNESDAY	THURSDAY	FRIDAY	SATURDAY
sit on toilet							
suppository							
breakfast							
enema							
sit on toilet							
BM in toilet							
soiling							
Week #___							
sit on toilet							
suppository							
breakfast							
enema							
sit on toilet							
BM in toilet							
soiling							

1. To empty the impacted bowel initially, give your child an enema (Fleet enemas are premixed and easy to use). If he does not respond with a bowel movement, give him another enema 1 hour later.
2. Once the bowel has been cleared, give your child a dose of mineral oil each day. This will produce loose stools that he will not be able to withhold. A recommended starting dose is 1½ ounces per 10 pounds of body weight. So if your child is 30 pounds, give him 4½ ounces of mineral oil, or ask your doctor for a recommended dosage. Divide this dosage in two, giving one-half in the morning, and one-half at bedtime. (A sweetened fruit drink or a piece of hard candy given after the medication will help your child get rid of the oily feeling in his mouth.) Do not give the mineral oil to a struggling, resistant child. This could result in aspiration and ultimately pneumonitis.

   If you find your child leaking oil during the day, it means that he is still holding solid feces. Slowly increase his mineral oil dosage a bit to see if the leaking stops. (Most pediatricians recommend that children who take mineral oil should also take multivitamins. Ask your doctor about this.)
3. Establish a routine of sitting on the toilet for about 10 minutes after breakfast and again after dinner (and, of course, whenever your child feels the need to defecate). If he is sitting up on a toilet seat, give him a footstool so that his feet can push down during defecation.
4. Encourage your child's cooperation by giving him verbal praise and by offering him a small snack or other treat each time he sits on the toilet.
5. Continue using the mineral oil and routine toilet sitting for three or four months until a pattern of regular bowel movements has been established. At this time the colon will have returned to its normal size, and it will have regained its ability to function properly on its own.
6. Withdraw the use of the mineral oil over a four- to eight-week period.
7. Adjust your child's diet to include foods high in fiber and fluids, and reduce his intake of binding

foods and milk (reduce to 1 pint each day). This
will help prevent a recurrence of the constipation.
8. When the mineral oil is completely phased out,
continue to prompt your child to use the toilet on
a regular basis.

Approaches #1 and #2 for encopresis differ in their
procedures, but they both work toward the same goal of
helping your child attain mature toileting habits and putting an end to his chronic constipation. These treatment
programs are difficult only in their demand for absolute
consistency. You can't implement a toilet routine on some
days, but not on others. You can't use a program for three
weeks, and then stop for a while because your in-laws are
visiting you. If you are committed to helping your child
stop his soiling, you must talk it over with your child, gain
the support of your spouse, and make up your mind to
follow through no matter who comes to visit, or where you
go on vacation, or how early in the morning you'll have
to get up to complete the procedure.

Before committing yourself to a program, however,
remember that it is a treatment procedure for children
who suffer chronic constipation and have lost full control
of their bowel function. (This is the most common type
of encopresis.) If your child was once bowel toilet
trained, and then regressed to soiling after experiencing
a period of great stress, this may not be an appropriate
treatment plan. If you feel that a new and stressful occurrence (a new sibling, house, or school; divorce, sepa-
ration, or death) has caused your child to regress to
pants soiling, and the soiling has lasted for more than
four weeks, it's a good idea to try the strategy explained
on page 115 that specifically addresses this situation before trying the second approach.

It may also be best to delay intensive encopresis treatment if you feel your child's personality type is the cause
of his soiling. Some children are a bit immature and
simply forget to use the toilet, or they ignore the urge
to defecate because they are busy playing. You may be
able to help this kind of child by following the simpler
program on page 131, which is intended for children who
are mildly delayed in their bowel training. That program
is primarily for the child who doesn't want to use the

toilet for his BMs. It does not use external aids for the relief of chronic constipation.

Occasionally, a child who is exceptionally stubborn or rebellious will continuously soil his pants as a deliberate act of defiance. He shows no signs of constipation, nor does he appear forgetful or overly involved in his play activities. This kind of child needs family counseling to discover the underlying cause of his soiling.

If you can eliminate stress and personality factors as the cause of your child"s persistent soiling, then the treatment programs we've discussed will be most effective in helping your child gain complete, voluntary bowel control. If you find it difficult to follow the program consistently, you may need the help, support, and supervision of a trained professional, such as a child psychologist. Call your state or county psychological association for a referral to someone trained in encopresis management.

Eric's Story (as Told by His Mom):

"Eric is an active, intelligent, happy boy who has lots of friends. He was toilet trained for urine and BMs by age two and one half, but shortly after his third birthday, I noticed that he seemed to be constipated quite often. Because it hurt him to pass the large hard stools, he would try to hold back, and he would have a bowel movement only every three days. On the days in between, I would see him twisting his body in crazy positions trying to hold in his BMs.

"When Eric was four, he continued to have trouble passing his stools, and he often complained of stomachaches. Sometimes I would see blood in the toilet when he did have a bowel movement, and I started noticing that his underwear was often soiled.

"When Eric turned five, he still suffered from constipation, but now I was very confused because he would soil his pants every day. This made no sense to me, and I often punished him severely. But the soiling, withholding, and constipation continued.

"My pediatrician said there was no physical reason for Eric's problem, although he did note that Eric had a history of constipation since infancy. He suggested that we try an encopresis treatment program [Approach #1] that had been developed by a psychologist.

"We began by changing Eric's diet. We included more fiber-rich foods like stewed prunes and raw fruit, and he began to drink six cups of water or juice each day.

"We also made a few changes in the program. We decided to do the toileting procedure at dinnertime (rather than breakfast time as suggested) because since both Eric's father and I work, the mornings are very hectic in our house. As prescribed by our doctor, we also added to the program a tablespoon of mineral oil in the morning and evening.

"We explained the program to Eric and gave him some responsibility for making it work. He kept track of his progress on the progress chart we kept in the bathroom. At the end of each week he could trade in his stars for a special treat or activity. He also took complete responsibility for cleaning up after himself when he soiled his pants.

"Establishing a structured toileting routine took some getting used to, but once we all became familiar with what was involved, and how it worked to solve the problem, we were able to follow through without too much difficulty.

"On the first night of the program, Eric needed two enemas because his bowel was so impacted. Then he passed three cups of feces. The rest of the week looked like this:

Eric's Progress

	Mon.	Tues.	Wed.	Thurs.	Fri.	Sat.	Sun.
PM toileting	✓	✓	✓	✓	✓	✓	✓
suppository	✓	✓	✓	✓	✓	✓	✓
dinner	✓	✓	✓	✓	✓	✓	✓
toilet	✓	✓	✓	✓	✓	✓	✓
enema	2	1	—	—	2	—	substitute suppository
BM	7:10	7:30	7:00	7:15	7:45	7:00	9:00
soiling	NO ★	NO ★	NO ★	NO ★	NO ★	NO ★	YES 2 TIMES!

(Eric traded in his stars for a night at the movies with his dad.)

"During the second week, Eric needed two suppositories each day, but no enemas to have a daily bowel movement. He was even starting to pass BMs in the toilet during the day when it wasn't time yet for the evening toileting procedure.

"During the third week, Eric still didn't need any enemas, and we used suppositories only twice. From the fourth week on, I eliminated all external aids, and he continued to have daily bowel movements without any soiling incidents.

"After two months on the program, we began to phase out the use of the mineral oil, and eliminated it completely during the third month.

"It's been six months since Eric started the treatment program. He is still on a fiber-rich diet; he still drinks lots of water and juice each day; he is still on a schedule of regular toileting times, and best of all, he is still having daily bowel movements and he no longer soils his pants. We're not keeping a progress chart anymore, because now Eric knows that daily bowel movements and proper diet are all a part of being a grown-up."

Chapter Eleven

Helping Children with Delayed Bladder Control

How to Help Children Three and a Half to Five Years Old Gain Daytime Bladder Control

Almost all children are completely daytime bladder trained using traditional training methods by the age of four. If the kinds of methods outlined in the Readiness Approach (page 54) have not been successful in training your child, however, the following methods for delayed bladder control will be helpful.

Treatment Approach #1: General Bladder Control Strategies

1. Check with your doctor to be sure there is no medical problem, such as a urinary tract infection, that may be causing the wetting.
2. Make a habit of checking for dryness and calculating when your child's bladder is likely to be full. When your child wakes up dry from a nap, or is dry for two consecutive hours, take him to the potty or toilet.
3. If at all possible, keep your child in diapers until there is some sign of a successful toileting routine. A child who is put into training pants or underwear

before he has had any success at using the toilet or potty is being set up for a constant failure and will feel disgraced when his parents realize he should go back into diapers.

4. Lower your expectations; anticipate only gradual improvement. Remember: Learning to use the toilet is a gradual process even for older children.

5. Some children want to urinate into the potty or toilet, but once they sit down, they can't relax the urethral sphincter muscle. You can try to help your child relax this muscle by:

• Tickling him while he's on the potty or toilet. Especially in girls this often relaxes the sphincter muscle enough to let out a spurt of urine and give the child a feeling of success.

• Giving him a warm bath before he sits on the potty or toilet.

• Giving him an enema to release feces. This tends to relax the bladder sphincter muscle and release urine as well as BMs.

• Running the water faucet while your child is on the potty or toilet. The sound of running water has been known to help children relax and urinate.

• Teaching him muscle training through exercises. You have the ability to stop and start your urine flow; show your child how you do this. Explain to him that he can also do it by tightening, then loosening the muscle that holds back the urine. Open and close your hand to give an example of how muscles can open and close. Children who strengthen their urethral sphincter muscle will have greater control over it when they urinate.

6. You can help your child gain bladder control by increasing his sensory awareness of urinating. Remove his diaper and let him play in the nude or in light underwear. Stay outdoors, weather permitting, to ease the cleanup burden, or stay on a washable floor at the times when you expect him to urinate.

When urine falls into a diaper, a child may not fully realize what has happened. But if he can see the urine and feel the wetness of it, he will more easily understand what you're talking about.

Approach #2: Scheduled Toileting

This program of remedial bladder training is adapted from a procedure that was developed and successfully implemented by Glenn Richmond to improve the bladder control of developmentally slow children.[1] It is easily adapted to help all children who have trouble attaining bladder control. This is a four-week program of scheduled toileting.

1. Take your child to the potty or toilet as follows:
   Week #1—every 15 minutes
   Week #2—every 30 minutes
   Week #3—every hour
   Week #4—every 2 hours
2. Before having your child sit on the potty or toilet, inspect his pants for dryness. If the pants are dry and clean, praise him by stating exactly what you're happy about. ("How nice! Your pants are dry.") Then let him sit on the potty or toilet seat. If he then urinates into the bowl, reward him with praise and a liquid drink that he likes. (Liquids are used as positive reinforcement and to increase the frequency of urination.)

   If his pants are wet or soiled, use Penalties 1 and 2 on page 121—expression of verbal disapproval and cleanliness training. Then proceed to toilet sitting. Reward him with praise and desired liquids if he urinates.
3. Stay calm and casual at all times.
4. Continue this procedure consistently for four weeks. By the end of the fourth week, your child should be accustomed to urinating in the potty or toilet. Begin to phase out the rewards, but continue to practice the penalty sequence for wetting. If, at the end of four weeks, your child is still not using the potty or toilet properly, it is probably due to a generally resistant attitude toward toilet training. See page 125 for the appropriate retraining approach.

How to Help Children Over Five Years Old Gain Daytime Bladder Control

Don't be alarmed if your child is over the age of five and yet occasionally comes home with wet pants. Sometimes even older children will lose control of their bladder sphincter muscle, especially in times of excitement, illness, or stress. This intermittent regression is to be expected, and it should not be confused with *enuresis,* which is a condition marked by persistent involuntary urination by a child over five years of age.

In some cases enuresis may be caused by a physical problem. Before you start a remedial training program, explain the situation to your pediatrician. Ask whether there is any factor in your child's health history that could cause this problem, and ask for a checkup if

- your child experiences pain or burning while urinating
- the urine stream dribbles out
- your child has an excessive need for fluids
- there is great frequency and/or urgency in urination
- your child cannot voluntarily stop or start the stream of urine

If there is no physical reason for your child's persistent daytime wetting, you can assume that he is probably wetting out of habit. Many children with daytime enuresis tend to ignore the urge to urinate when they are deeply involved in play activities or they wet their pants because they are immature and simply forget to use the toilet when they feel the sensation of a full bladder.

Treatment

The first treatment method you should try is one that is simple and direct:

- Remind your child to use the toilet frequently throughout the day.

- Watch for bodily signs (crotch holding, leg squeezing, dancing around) that your child has to urinate and then take him to the toilet without allowing time for excuses or delay tactics.
- Keep a record of when he has to urinate. Wetting often occurs at approximately the same time each day. If you can discover the probable time of wetting, that's when you should call him in to use the toilet.
- Offer praise when he urinates into the toilet.
- Offer rewards when he goes to the bathroom without prompting.

If this simple approach doesn't work, you can try the more intensive program for mildly delayed children who have trouble attaining daytime bladder control (see page 157). Since the majority of children who have daytime wetting also suffer from bed-wetting, however, you may upset your child by trying to train him to control both day and nighttime wetting at the same time. Studies have found that when children master their nighttime wetting problem, the daytime control may follow. So, if you plan to help your child gain nighttime bladder control, use the simple program for daytime control outlined previously, and concentrate your remedial efforts on the nighttime problem.

Chapter Twelve

Helping Children with Bed-Wetting

How to Help Children Three and a Half to Five Years Old Stop Bed-Wetting

The average age at which children attain nighttime bladder control is thirty-three months. Statistics aside, however, the nighttime bladder control of children between the ages of three and a half to five years is often an on-again-off again situation. As explained in Chapter Three, nighttime bladder control for young children is often a matter of bladder maturation rather than training per se. When a child's bladder matures to the point where it can hold urine for 8 hours, he will stay dry at night. This usually happens after daytime bladder control is mastered, and it is evident when a child consistently wakes in the morning with dry diapers or pants. It is expected that nighttime control will be achieved by most children by the time they are six years of age. If it is not, the intensive nighttime toileting routine explained in this chapter may be necessary to control this bed-wetting problem.

Although mildly delayed nighttime bladder control is not uncommon, nor even abnormal, it can still be a very distressing situation for children and their parents. Children who are daytime bladder trained, for example, may not want to wear "babyish" diapers to bed. Many of these mildly delayed children feel embarrassed and ashamed. Some even begin to withdraw from their family and friends. Obviously, this is a difficult situation that needs attention. Parents, too, tend to feel frustrated and even angered by nighttime wetting. It's inconvenient; it disrupts their sleep if the child wakes, finds himself wet, and calls to be changed; it's extra work to continuously clean the mattress and sheets; and it's also tiring to fight the nighttime battle to put the child in diapers continually.

While you're waiting for your child to outgrow nighttime wetting (which happens by adolescence in 98 percent of the population) here are some tips that may help you and your child live with the problem:

- Remain calm. Your anger and disapproval will only further shame and embarrass your child about something over which he has little or no control. A negative and/or punitive parental attitude will *not* stop nighttime wetting.
- Consider your family history. Bed-wetting is often a family trait. Did you or your spouse, or an aunt or uncle, or someone else in the family ever have this problem? If so, tell your child about it; it will help him realize that it is not his fault and it will show him that many people do outgrow the problem.
- Keep your child's room comfortably warm at night (65–70°). Children urinate more often when they are cold.
- Limit your child's fluid intake in the late evening, especially fluids that can irritate the bladder such as orange juice and caffeine drinks like colas, coffee, or tea. (Don't overdo it, though, by starting to restrict fluids in the late afternoon. Children need fluids in their bodies.)
- Make sure your child empties his bladder just before he goes to sleep and again immediately upon waking.
- Adapt the environment to make it easy for him to get up and go to the bathroom if he feels the urge. Keep the room temperature comfortable. Put a

night-light in his room and in the bathroom. Be sure the way to the bathroom is lit. Give him pajamas that are easily managed during sleepy toileting.

- Wake your child and bring him to the bathroom every hour until you go to bed. This will assure an empty bladder and reduce the length of time he must retain urine.

- You can try to motivate your child by offering him small rewards for dry nights. This usually meets with limited success, however, because most children at this age do not have control over their bedwetting. It may, in fact, put pressure on him and draw undue attention to his problem.

- Express confidence that he will soon stop wetting the bed.

- Wait it out. Some parents are content to wait patiently for nighttime bladder control. If you do that, you can help ease the strain and frustration of nighttime wetting by making a few bedtime adjustments.

If your child rarely wakes up dry in the morning, continue to use diapers. If your child resists wearing them, explain that the wetting is not his fault during sleep because, unlike during the daytime, he has no control of the urine that leaks out. Then assure him that soon he will be able to stay dry at night and won't need diapers. If your child wakes up dry most mornings, let him wear training pants to bed if he wants to. Be sure to send him to the potty or toilet the first thing each morning and praise him every time his diaper or pants are dry when he wakes.

Protect your child's mattress. You can do this in a number of ways: You can buy rubberized flannel sheets or plastic mattress covers or you can put down a plastic sheet (a shower curtain or plastic tablecloth will do) under the bed sheet. Another method is to wrap a thick towel across the center of the bed. If your child wets, you can remove the towel and lay him on the dry sheet beneath. Yet another plan is to keep a sleeping bag on the floor next to your child's bed. If he wets in the night, he can jump into the sleeping bag without disturbing you. Also, keep dry pajamas nearby, and leave a plastic bag or hamper in the room for easy deposit of wet clothing.

These nighttime toileting tips should help you and your young child deal with the problem of bed-wetting. If your child continues to wet his bed after he is five years old, however, it may be necessary to use one of the intensive nighttime toileting routines discussed in the next section.

How to Help Children Over Five Years Old Stop Bed-Wetting

Nighttime bed-wetting after the age of five years is called *nocturnal enuresis*. Children with primary enuresis have never attained a substantial period of night dryness, and those with secondary enuresis had achieved nighttime control of their bladder for at least one year, but then relapsed and resumed bed-wetting.

Whether your child's bed-wetting problem is primary or secondary in nature, it is probably an upsetting situation for both of you. You may find some comfort in the following statistics that document how common it is for children to be bed wetters:

- About 5 million school-age children persistently wet their beds.
- Twenty to 25 percent of all five-year-olds wet their beds.
- Boys wet their beds twice as often as girls.
- Ten percent of six- to ten-year-olds wet their beds.
- About 2 percent of American soldiers in World War II wet the bed.
- Night wetting was recognized as a medical problem by the Egyptians in 1550 B.C, and it was written about in the first English-language book for pediatricians.[1]

Although nocturnal enuresis is a common occurrence, it is only recently that effective treatments have been developed. Older and crueler remedies that proved ineffective included tying a string around the child's penis, pouring cold streams of water over a child's spine, making the bed wetter sit on a hot stove, and forcing him to drink a pint of his own urine. In 1535, Hollis Phaer, the father of modern pediatrics, customarily prescribed ground-up hedge-hog testicles, while his colleagues often recommended drinking the urine of spayed swine. Later in the nineteenth century, mattresses with steel spikes and frames were invented to solve the problem. Some practitioners even tried to stop night wetting by cauterizing the child's urethra with silver nitrate.

Home remedies such as raising the foot or head of the bed, having the child sleep on his back, sleeping on a knot, sleeping on the floor, and drinking a variety of home-brewed potions, have been popular modes of treatment over the years. Also common were harsh punishments such as beating, scalding, and whipping; and demeaning penalties such as making the child spend the day in his wet pants, and hanging his wet sheets out the window as a sign of shame.

All of these remedies have proven unsuccessful in solving the bed-wetting problem and many families are left without recourse when their pediatricians advise them to let the child grow out of it. Although it's true that 98 percent of nocturnal enuresis cases disappear without any form of treatment by the time the child reaches late adolescence, that is of little consolation for the many thousands of parents and children who have lived with this problem for years. I've received many letters and phone calls from parents who are confused and upset by this problem. Their concerns may sound familiar to you:

"I have had my son checked by three pediatricians and one urologist. The first three doctors said to wait for him to outgrow his bed-wetting. The urologist recommended pills, which we tried for five days, but I didn't like the mood changes in my son. Am I doing enough by doing nothing?"

"My family doctor told me not to worry when I asked about my six-year-old's bed-wetting problem. He said this would take care of itself. Well, it hasn't and now my son is ten. I want him to know what it's like to wake up in a dry bed and with dry underwear and what fun it is to sleep over at his friends' homes. Please give us some advice. I desperately need it. It is very difficult not being able to talk about this with anyone who knows what it is like."

"My four-year-old son is still not toilet trained in the day or night, and my eight-year-old son is still wetting the bed every night. I feel I have tried everything, with no success, so they are both still in diapers. Neither one likes the diapers. Should I continue to use them?"

"My concern is about my ten-year-old son who has never been dry at night. This appears to be due to heredity as his father and uncle were both bed wetters. My pediatrician has advised waiting for bladder maturation, but now my son has joined the Cub Scouts and wants to go camping. I can't let him go as long as the wetting persists. What should I do?"

These letters and hundreds more like them make it clear that, although enuresis will usually resolve itself over time, there are many valid reasons to treat the problem. Some of them are:

- Bed-wetting as a source of ongoing parent/child conflicts.
- Bed-wetting as a source of constant embarrassment to the child.
- Bed-wetting as a source of low self-esteem.
- Children who wet their beds usually do not want to go to sleep-away camp, overnight parties, or even enjoy a night spent at a friend's house.
- There is a 50/50 chance that a five-year-old who has nocturnal enuresis will still be wetting his bed at the age of twelve.

All of these problems can usually be resolved within two or three months with a bed-wetting treatment program. It makes sense, therefore, to help your child conquer bed-wetting, rather than wait for him to grow out of it.

What's the Problem?

There are several known reasons why older children may have difficulty attaining nighttime bladder control:

- Some have immature sleep patterns, which means the arousal patterns that would allow them to awaken during light (REM) sleep in response to the feeling of a full bladder are not well developed. If you can move, undress, and disturb your child with noise without waking him, you can suspect this condition may be the cause of nighttime wetting.
- Stress caused by changes in a child's life or illness.
- Heredity. According to a new Danish study, many children older than age six who have never achieved through-the-night dryness may be born with a specific genetic marker that has been linked to bed-wetting. This marker is passed down from either or both parents. Earlier research has shown that if one parent was a bed-wetter then a child has a 44 percent chance of being one, too. If both parents were, then there is a 77 percent chance that the child will be a bed-wetter also. If both parents were not bed-wetters, their children have only a 15 percent chance of becoming chronic bed wetters.

Consider Physical Causes

The following treatment for nighttime wetting is not an appropriate way to treat children who suffer from a physical problem. Medical illness, such as urinary tract infections, sickle-cell anemia, diabetes, or chronic constipation (which enlarges the child's rectum, causing it to press on his bladder) can cause bed-wetting. Food allergies, too, have been known to contribute to enuresis. Also, a deficiency of the antidiuretic hormone (ADH), which decreases urine output during sleep, can cause a child to wet at night.

Before you begin the following remedial approach, check with your pediatrician to be sure that there is no physical reason for your child's bed-wetting.

Consider Emotional Causes

Secondary enuresis may be caused by emotional, stress-related problems that should be explored before you begin the program outlined in this chapter.

Stress is a part of everyday life, so it takes a bit of detective work to find out if stress is the trigger for bed-wetting, especially in a child who was sleeping dry through the night and then reverted to wetting. Stress can come from exciting sources like traveling, a birthday, a visit from a relative, the beginning of school, or the birth of a sibling. It also stems from upsetting events or situations like illness, hospitalization, family arguments, divorce, a death in the family, a frightening movie, an overbearing teacher, or a class bully.

If you suspect that your child's bed-wetting may be sparked by stress, address the problem at the root first, before you spend time treating the symptom of the wet bed. Talk with teachers, day-care providers, and others who are in contact with him. Talk with your child. It may take a few conversations, so don't be impatient. Remain open to what he has to say, and try to get him to tell you what's on his mind. If you can identify a problem, deal with it directly, and in many cases the nighttime wetting will stop.

If you are unable to pinpoint the source of stress (although you know your child is upset about something), or if you have difficulty helping your child deal with whatever is bothering him, then you should seek professional counseling from a competent counselor who can help your child manage the stress and end the bed-wetting.

Preparation for Bed-Wetting Treatment

Once you're sure your child's bed-wetting is not caused by physical or emotional problems, take some time to prepare yourself and your child for this new approach to bed-wetting.

Rally Support

Before you begin remedial training, discuss the program with any other adult caretakers in your home. All of you will need to offer support and encouragement to your child, as well as supervision of his efforts to follow the program.

It's also important that you clearly understand that it is not your child's fault that he wets the bed. He is not being lazy, or disobedient, or stubborn. His bed-wetting is most likely not a conscious or voluntary act. Most children who do not attain bladder control by the age of six years are delayed in this function because of an immaturity in the neuromuscular development of their bladder. About two-thirds of children who are primary enuretics have relatives who were bed wetters. It seems that bed-wetting is often an inherited trait. Also noteworthy is the finding that four out of five older children who wet their beds are normal and well-adjusted.

Talk to Your Child

As you begin this program, keep in mind that bed-wetting is a developmental problem, not a behavioral one. The majority of kids who have primary enuresis do not have it as a result of psychological problems. However, experts agree that bed-wetting could become an emotional or behavioral problem if during this period the child is treated in an abusive or negligent way.

Before you begin remedial training, you should also talk to your child about the program. Its success depends in large part on his inner motivation to stop wetting, his belief that he can control the wetting, and on his ability to take personal responsibility for the wetting. The more facts your child knows about the causes of his wetting and the possibility of an effective remedy for bed-wetting, the more likely he is to cooperate and be an active partner in the treatment.

Two types of bed-wetting programs are explained in this chapter for children over five years old. The Basic Approach is a method based on behavioral conditioning that has helped stop night wetting in many children who have used it. The second approach is a more intensive method that utilizes a mechanical urine alarm in addition to the procedure of the Basic Approach.

Basic Approach to Bed-Wetting

Preparation

The information that was given on pages 162–165 for handling younger children with bed-wetting problems is still appropriate for your older child. Read through this section again for tips on adapting the bedroom environment for easy toileting and on protecting your child's mattress.

Nightly Routine

Create a series of rituals that will get your child into the habit of nighttime toileting. You might supervise his routine of activities like washing his face, brushing his teeth, and urinating in the toilet. Then you can put him to bed in a calm state by talking about the good day that's passed, or reading a happy story. This will help him sleep with a sense of security and safety and lessen the chances of stress-induced bed-wetting.

Retention Control

Bed-wetting occurs when the bladder sphincter muscle involuntarily relaxes during sleep. Studies have found that children can strengthen the sphincter muscle to hold back urine for longer periods of time, and they can also train the bladder to hold greater amounts of urine. Some children who feel a need to urinate too frequently are in the habit of emptying the bladder before it is actually full. A child who is five years of age or older should urinate only about four to six times a day. You can check how much urine your child's bladder is holding before signaling the urge to urinate by asking him to urinate into a measuring cup. Record the amount of urine he passes. He should be able to hold one or more ounces per year of age—that is, a six-year-old should void at least 6 ounces of urine. This information is helpful in teaching bladder control because if, for example, a six-year-old insists he needs to urinate but then voids only 2 ounces of urine, his parents will know that his bladder was probably not full and he needs to strengthen the urethral sphincter muscle. Children can increase their bladder capacity and strengthen the sphincter muscle by following these suggestions.

- Give your child extra fluids during the day. Then whenever he has to urinate, ask him to hold off for 2 or 3 minutes before voiding. If he feels he can't hold off and gets upset, try making a game of it, or distract him with a short story, or offer him stars for every minute he can hold off, and then let him trade in the stars for a toy. When he is able to hold off for 2 or 3 minutes with no problems, ask him to hold off for an additional 2 to 3 minutes until he is gradually able to wait 15 minutes. After a month or two he should be able to hold off for 30 minutes. During the rest of this program, remind him to hold off for 30 minutes when he first feels the urge to urinate. This will train his bladder to hold more urine before feeling full, and it will also improve his muscle resistance to bladder contractions.

- While your child is urinating, ask him to stop the stream of urine by tightening the sphincter muscle, and then start the stream again by relaxing the muscle. Once he feels comfortable doing this, urge him to do it several times with each urination. This exercise will improve his ability to control the sphincter muscle, and it will also strengthen the muscle's ability to hold back the urine during sleep.

Nighttime Toileting

Children often wet their beds because during sleep they don't respond to the internal signal of a full bladder. You can help your child get into the habit of waking at night to go to the bathroom.

Establish a getting-up routine by waking your child every hour between the time he goes to bed and the time you go to bed. When you wake him, make sure he is fully awake, since you don't want to encourage his habit of urinating in his sleep. Once he is awake, make him responsible for the following routine:

- Check the bed for dryness. If it is dry have your child mark a *D* for "dry" on the progress chart that he must keep by his bed. (See page 174 for the Basic Approach to Bed-wetting Progress Chart.)

Then give him a reward based on the Reward and Penalty system on page 120.

If the bed is wet, have your child mark a *W* on the progress chart, but do *not* follow the penalty procedure explained in the reward and penalty system. It is not appropriate for this bed-wetting program. Your child must, however, take responsibility for the wet bed. Have him (with your help when needed) change his wet clothes, sheets, and blankets; finish urinating in the toilet (do not carry him to the bathroom); and then get back into bed. He may also be able to help you wash the wet items in the morning. Repeat this procedure every hour until you go to bed, and then do it again in the morning. If, in the morning, you find that your child has been dry through the entire night, mark it on the chart and give him a special reward.

This waking routine will help your child get into the habit of waking to urinate; it will put the responsibility for wet nights on him; it will increase his chances of having dry nights, and these dry nights will give him the feel of success and motivate him to continue the program. All of this, combined with your supportive attitude, the nightly calming rituals, and the retention-control exercises, should teach your child to stay dry at night within two to three months.

If, after using this Basic Approach to Bed-wetting for three months, your child shows no signs of improvement, then it may be time to use a urine alarm while you continue using these basic strategies. This Combined Approach is explained in the next section.

Combined Approach

The urine alarm is a device that wakes a child when he urinates in his sleep. Its purpose is two-fold: The child will either learn to wake and go to the bathroom when the bladder begins to contract and puts pressure on the sphincter muscle, or he will learn to hold back his urine throughout the night.

A Nigerian tribe can probably be credited with inventing the first urine alarm system. If a child persisted in wetting during the night, the parent would tie a frog

Basic Approach to Bed-Wetting
Progress Chart

SUNDAY	MONDAY	TUESDAY	WEDNESDAY	THURSDAY	FRIDAY	SATURDAY
Wake-up D/W Time: | | |	Wake-up D/W Time: | | |	Wake-up D/W Time: | | |	Wake-up D/W Time:	Wake-up D/W Time: | | |	Wake-up D/W Time: | | |	Wake-up D/W Time: | | |
Wake-up D/W Time: | | |	Wake-up D/W Time:	Wake-up D/W Time: | | |	Wake-up D/W Time:	Wake-up D/W Time: | | |	Wake-up D/W Time: | | |	Wake-up D/W Time: | | |
Wake-up D/W Time: | | |	Wake-up D/W Time:	Wake-up D/W Time: | | |	Wake-up D/W Time:	Wake-up D/W Time: | | |	Wake-up D/W Time: | | |	Wake-up D/W Time: | | |
Wake-up D/W Time: | | |	Wake-up D/W Time:	Wake-up D/W Time: | | |	Wake-up D/W Time:	Wake-up D/W Time: | | |	Wake-up D/W Time: | | |	Wake-up D/W Time: | | |
Wake-up D/W Time: | | |	Wake-up D/W Time:	Wake-up D/W Time: | | |	Wake-up D/W Time:	Wake-up D/W Time: | | |	Wake-up D/W Time: | | |	Wake-up D/W Time: | | |

*Give incentives and let your child take responsibility
for his or her toileting*

to his penis. Then if the boy urinated, the frog would
jump and croak, thus waking him. Although the effectiveness of this frog and string method is not known, the
urine alarm method has been very successful over the
last 30 years in teaching children to stay dry through
the night.

The Process

When a child first starts to urinate, the urine activates an electrical circuit that sets off an alarm. The child must then:

- Get up immediately and turn off the alarm
- Go to the bathroom and finish urinating.
- Put dry bedding on his mattress
- Mark the time of his wetting on his progress chart (See the chart on page 178)

This procedure is direct and simple. When it is consistently followed without deviation, most children learn to stay dry through the night. Initially, the procedure is considered successful when the child sleeps through 14 consecutive nights with no wettings. At this point ask your child to drink a cup of water at bedtime and then see if he can stay dry for another two weeks. This procedure ensures that your child has really learned to control his urination at night. Some children learn to do this quickly, whereas others take as long as 4 months, but the average length of training time is between 8 to 12 weeks.

The Advantages of the Urine Alarm

- It is the method of bed-wetting control with the highest rate of success.
- It is a program of immediate feedback that encourages learning.
- A bed-wetting child does not sleep through the night with wet clothing and bedding.
- If a child has not been able to stop nighttime wetting by following the strategies of the Basic Approach, this method usually supplies the extra help he needs to learn to stay dry.

Disadvantages of the Urine Alarm

- The method has a relapse rate of 30 to 40 percent within six months of treatment. Many children need to repeat the procedure once or twice before they stay dry.
- The method must be followed *every* night during the training period. Some parents and children become frustrated and give up before achieving success. Before using this approach, you must resolve to continue the method for three or four months.
- Some children do not awaken at the sound of the alarm (although with some models, the rest of the household certainly does). Parents may have to be backup awakeners for the first week or two.

If you decide to use the urine alarm, prepare your child in advance. Explain how the device works and assure him that it can't hurt him or give him an electrical shock. Then discuss his role in turning off the alarm, going to the bathroom, changing the wet bedding, resetting the alarm, and keeping an accurate record of wettings on his progress chart.

Since the management of this device is usually done in a state of sleepiness, it will help if you give your child daily opportunities to practice using the bell and pad. Practice at bedtime, having your child lie on the bed with the pad in place. Activate the alarm in whatever manner works best with your particular device. When the alarm sounds, let your child make a game of quickly pouncing on the alarm to shut it off. (Immediate awakening is very important to the success of the method.) Then have him practice going to the bathroom, returning to the bedroom, resetting the alarm, changing the bedding, and recording the incident on the progress chart.

Repeat this practice run at least six times each evening at bedtime.

The Combined Approach to Bed-Wetting
Progress Chart

SUNDAY	MONDAY	TUESDAY	WEDNESDAY	THURSDAY	FRIDAY	SATURDAY
Time of Wet alarm: spot: |||	Time of Wet alarm: spot: |||	Time of Wet alarm: spot: |||	Time of Wet alarm: spot: |||	Time of Wet alarm: spot: |||	Time of Wet alarm: spot: |||	Time of Wet alarm: spot: |||
Time of Wet alarm: spot: |||	Time of Wet alarm: spot: |||	Time of Wet alarm: spot: |||	Time of Wet alarm: spot: |||	Time of Wet alarm: spot: |||	Time of Wet alarm: spot: |||	Time of Wet alarm: spot: |||
Time of Wet alarm: spot: |||	Time of Wet alarm: spot: |||	Time of Wet alarm: spot: |||	Time of Wet alarm: spot: |||	Time of Wet alarm: spot: |||	Time of Wet alarm: spot: |||	Time of Wet alarm: spot: |||
Time of Wet alarm: spot: |||	Time of Wet alarm: spot: |||	Time of Wet alarm: spot: |||	Time of Wet alarm: spot: |||	Time of Wet alarm: spot: |||	Time of Wet alarm: spot: |||	Time of Wet alarm: spot: |||
Time of Wet alarm: spot: |||	Time of Wet alarm: spot: |||	Time of Wet alarm: spot: |||	Time of Wet alarm: spot: |||	Time of Wet alarm: spot: |||	Time of Wet alarm: spot: |||	Time of Wet alarm: spot: |||

Once you begin this Combined Approach, you'll find your child's progress advances in four stages:

- In the first stage, the frequency of urination will remain the same, or perhaps even increase.
- In the second stage, the frequency of wetting will decrease; the alarm will ring at a later hour as the child begins to hold back longer, and the average size of the wet spot on his bed will become smaller (often only a few inches in diameter) as he learns to wake and stop urinating immediately at the sound of the alarm. In this second stage, the child may eventually awaken to urinate before wetting and sounding the alarm.
- In the third stage, the child will awaken before wetting the bed with increasing frequency. He will finally attain dry nights, but will continue to sleep with the pad.
- In the fourth stage, the child will sleep without the pad. He may still awaken for longer periods until eventually he sleeps through the night without waking or wetting. This stage can last for a few weeks to several months.

The Combined Approach is a highly effective way to stop persistent bed-wetting. Some parents find it difficult to manage the program in a consistent manner for an extended period of time, however, so they drop out before achieving success. For this reason, it seems best to use the urine alarm along with professional counseling. In fact, studies show a marked improvement in the method's success rate when it is used under the guidance of a trained counselor. Call your state or county psychological association and ask for a therapist who is trained in treating enuresis with a urine alarm.

A number of different bell and pad devices are available on the market. Most of them cost about $40. You can buy one from the sources listed in Appendix A.

Alternate Treatments for Bed-Wetting

Hypnosis

Some bed-wetting children have attained night dryness through a program of hypnosis. Studies on this approach to bed-wetting, however, remain inconclusive in determining its overall effectiveness. If you are interested in this method, call your state or county psychological association and ask for a referral to a therapist who uses hypnosis for treatment of enuresis.

Drugs

Drug therapy can be an effective treatment for enuresis, but only in special circumstances and always with caution. Drugs offer quick results, but once stopped, a large percentage of children return to bed-wetting. Many professionals will discourage the use of drug therapy for your child, especially if it is requested because of its "easy" and quick application to this chronic problem.

Imipramine (Tofranil, SK-Pramine, Janimine, or Imavate), has been commonly used to treat bed-wetting, but it is not recommended by the American Academy of Pediatrics. It is a toxic drug and an antidepressant that can cause unpleasant side effects including dizziness, anorexia, irritability, cardiac irregularities, and difficulty in falling asleep. Overdoses have been known to cause death in young children. The medication must be carefully monitored and stored in a safe place.

Desmopressin acetate (DDAVP) is now available in nasal spray for the treatment of enuresis. DDAVP is a synthetic version of the antidiuretic hormone, ADH. Normally, the level of ADH rises at night, signaling the kidney to regulate and slow urine production. Studies in Denmark have shown that bed-wetting children often don't experience that ADH increase and produce an abnormally high amount of urine at night, inevitably leading to bed-wetting. DDAVP suppresses the kidneys from making urine, thus decreasing the likelihood of bed-wetting. Like all drugs, DDAVP comes with side effects, most commonly an occasional headache, nosebleed, or nasal irritation. It is not to be used by children with cystic fibrosis, nasal polyps, epilepsy, or heart or kidney disease. This drug is very expensive; relapse rates after use is discontinued are high, and cannot be recommended as long-term therapy.

In some cases, drug therapy can be used successfully on a short-term basis or to suppress bed-wetting while a child is at camp or on vacation. In the long run, however, drugs alone are not the solution to bed-wetting for most children.

Keith's Story (as Told by His Mom):

"My seven-year-old son, Keith, does not wet his bed at night. One year ago, I never thought I'd be able to say that. Keith had never learned to stay dry at night, and by the age of six, his dad and I were concerned that he would have an ongoing problem (his dad was a bed wetter until the age of twelve).

"Although we weren't sure how to help Keith, we wanted to do something because he was becoming very upset by his night wetting, and he wanted to go away to summer camp. I didn't think there was an emotional or physical problem because he wasn't under any unusual stress, and he didn't wet during the day. But we still thought it would be best to start looking for an answer with a visit to our pediatrician. Keith had never had any major illness; he had not been hospitalized, and he had no neurological or physical handicaps. As we expected, our doctor found no physical reason for his wetting.

"We spent the next six months trying a number of remedies. We began by lifting him in his sleep to urinate just before we went to bed at midnight. We restricted his fluid intake in the evening. We tried shaming him by calling bed-wetting "babyish." Nothing worked, and we were forced to put Keith back into diapers at night.

"Then Keith's pediatrician prescribed the drug Tofranil, which he hoped would stop the wetting. After one month we stopped using it because it didn't help Keith's bed-wetting at all, but it gave him a skin rash, and it made him irritable and sleepless.

"Since Keith's dad had a history of allergic reactions

to milk, we thought that maybe Keith's wetting might be a type of allergy. So with nothing to lose, we tried a restricted diet that eliminated wheat, milk, corn, pork, eggs, and chocolate. This had no effect on Keith's wetting.

"Finally, we went to a child psychologist. He made Keith feel much better when he assured him that he knew Keith wasn't wetting because of stubbornness, hostility, or babyish tendencies. He said that the wetting was most likely due to a delay in the development of his sphincter muscle control, and so we began our new program of nighttime bladder training with sphincter muscle exercises. (In the beginning, Keith's bladder could only hold 3 to 4 ounces of urine during the day. When we finished this program, he could hold 5 to 7 ounces. He also decreased the number of times he had to urinate each day from an average of seven, to five.)

"In addition to the exercises, we agreed to use a urine alarm. This device would wake Keith whenever he began to urinate at night. I agreed to be his backup awakener if he slept through the alarm. We practiced how to use it until Keith felt comfortable with the whole routine. Then feeling optimistic (and at the same time hesitant since we'd been let down so many times before) we committed ourselves to giving the program a try for three months.

"Keith was put in charge of cleaning the pad part of the urine alarm and putting it in a dry pillowcase each time he wet. He also made up a progress chart, and his dad and I promised him a new skateboard when he went one week without wetting. This chart helped us keep track of when we would buy Keith a skateboard, but it also helped us see the subtle signs of success, like the increasing time between wettings and the shrinking size of the wet spots.

"During the first four nights, our progress chart looked like this:

alarm	wet spot	alarm	wet spot	alarm	wet spot	alarm	wet spot
9:30	20"	10:10	24"	10:00	8"	9:40	10"
3:20	12"	2:10	15"	4:00	6"	12:30	★

"On the fourth night, Keith woke on his own at 12:30, and went to the bathroom. For the first time, he beat the alarm. For the next two weeks, Keith's progress zigzagged back and forth from wet nights to dry nights. In the third week, he slept dry through the night two times.

"By week five and six, Keith was not wetting at all so we began what the doctor called "overlearning." Keith drank a glass of water just before going to bed. During weeks seven and eight, Keith did not wet his bed at all, even though he had the extra fluid in him. Sometimes he would wake himself to go to the bathroom, and sometimes he would sleep dry right through the night.

"We removed the urine alarm from Keith's bed and crossed our fingers. After all these years of trying different things, it seemed too much to hope for that Keith was really in total control of his bladder after only two months of training. That was six weeks ago, and Keith is still completely dry every morning.

"Not only does Keith have a new skateboard, he has a better self-image, a more pleasant personality, and the comfort of a dry mattress and a good night's sleep."

If bed wetting continues past the ages of seven to eight years, or if it interferes with a child's adjustment—his own self-image, his ability to relate to his peers, or his ability to see himself as a successful person—it is time to seek a consultation with a child psychologist who is skilled in these issues. This kind of assistance could support and encourage him during this important time in his development.

PART III

Special Circumstances

Chapter Thirteen

Training with a Care-giver

There's no doubt about it, children need 'round-the-clock help while they're toilet training. If your child spends part of his day with a care-giver, then this person needs to be part of your toilet-training team. The most valuable thing you and the caregiver can bring to this training period is a cooperative attitude.

Of course, there are a variety of child-care arrangements. Your child may be training with an in-home nanny or sitter, with a relative, with someone who watches a few children in her own home, or with a staff member of a larger day-care center. In each of these situations, the exact details of toilet training will be individualized to meet your child's and the caregiver's needs, but regardless of where your child is being trained, there are a few guidelines that will ease your child (and you) through the process.

Before You Start

Three-year-old Henry was finally toilet trained! For three weeks he had been wearing "big-boy" underpants and had very few accidents. His mom, Cari, was ready to pat herself on the back for getting through a relatively easy training experience when everything abruptly turned around.

"Henry started doing very strange things that caused a lot of arguments in our house," remembers

Cari. "He kept taking the potty seat out of the bathroom, for example, and putting it in the kitchen—that's not allowed in our house so I'd carry it right back." In the middle of the tantrum that followed, Henry would usually wet his pants. He also started forgetting to pour his urine from the potty bowl into the toilet and wash his hands. "Unless I yelled at him," says Cari, "he wouldn't do the things he knew he was supposed to do. I couldn't figure out what happened until I looked back and realized that the trouble started around the same time he started going to a new babysitter after his preschool class."

After a little investigating, Cari found out that at the babysitter's, the potty chair was in the kitchen and clean up and hygiene weren't part of the toileting routine. No wonder Henry was confused. It was time to have a long talk with the sitter.

It's important to let your child's care-giver know your method of toilet training, so she can reinforce what you're teaching your child—and also offer you guidance and encouragement. Many care-givers are seasoned veterans who have helped scores of children master this skill and may be able to help you coordinate at-home and at-day-care training.

Although care-givers are usually helpful allies in toilet training, sometimes there may be differences of opinion and there will be a need for some give-and-take negotiating on both sides. It's important to explain the toilet-training method you prefer before you start training. If the procedures are the same at home and with the care-giver, it will be easier for your child.

Get It Together

It may happen that you and the care-giver don't agree on how to best train your child. In this case, ideally, your training method should prevail. For instance, if the care-giver uses a firm training method requiring the children to sit on the toilet at certain scheduled times, and you prefer a flexible, child-directed schedule, she should follow your wishes. However, in a busy child-care center, the care-giver may not be able to use your preferred training method. In this case, make time to sit down and talk about the details of a training program you can both live with.

No one method is absolutely better than another. The most important point is that both you and the care-giver use the same method. Consistency lets your child know what is expected of him and it makes the process of toilet training a cooperative team effort rather than a battle of adult wills that hurts the child.

Tips for Training with a Care-giver

Regardless which method you choose, there are a few general training-with-a-care-giver tips that will make it easier to toilet train with multiple trainers:

- If your child is being trained at a child-care center, find out what kind of toilet seat adapter or potty chair the center has and use that same kind at home.
- Tell the care-giver the words your child is using to signal that she has to go. If you are using the term "urinating" and the care-giver is saying "wee-wee," your child will be confused.
- Discuss in advance how accidents are handled. The care-giver must know that you will absolutely not allow harsh punishments for accidents.
- Dress your child appropriately for training: easy-to-pull down pants and/or short dresses for girls.
- If you are using rewards as incentives (star charts, treats, stickers, etc.) make sure your care-giver doles them out as you'd like. And be sure you supply something that can be shared with all the children, like stickers or M&Ms. Most care-givers don't like to give treats to just one child in front of the others.
- Hygiene is especially important when a number of children use the toilet facilities. Make sure there is a sink for your child to wash his hands and make sure your child knows to use it. If you think hand-washing rules aren't being enforced at the center, complain.

Deadline Training

Some centers accept children only after they are toilet trained. This is an understandable requirement that is often necessary based on the type of licensing the center has and its inability to offer sanitary diapering conditions. However, this restriction can cause parents much distress and put far too much pressure on a child to train on a deadline. One little boy whose name had just come to the top of a waiting list for a much-desired "no-diapers" center was so pressured to use the toilet that his training took twice as long and was more traumatic than it should have been.

Don't rush toilet training to meet a deadline. It's better to find other child care until he's ready for a no-diapers center. And don't say he's ready when he's not. It's embarrassing for the child who has an accident in an unsympathetic environment and it's unsanitary to put him in a place that doesn't have proper conditions for diapering.

When your child is ready, you can then transfer him to a no-diapers center—but don't be surprised if your "completely trained" child has an accident when he first attends the new center. It's very likely there will be a relapse when your child is put in a new situation. Sometimes it happens for simple reasons like the fact that the center uses a different kind of toilet. Or, your child may forget his training because the schedule is new, or the center is unfamiliar, or he feels scared. Be understanding with your child and honest with the new care-giver. These accidents are temporary setbacks and nothing to worry about.

Chapter Fourteen

Training While Traveling or Away from Home

In most circumstances, it's best to stay close to home when you first begin toilet training. Choose a time when you know you won't be going on vacation, or visiting distant relatives, or even doing a lot of holiday shopping. A child's immature sphincter muscle is not entirely under his control, and certainly not for very long. When a toilet-training child says, "I have to go," he really has to go *now*. So prolonged periods in cars, trains, or shopping malls, or on the beach with a child in training pants are bound to result in messy accidents.

Elaine learned this the hard way. Her 27-month-old Maggie had been toilet training for several weeks and rarely had any accidents. Confident that her daughter could now stay dry like any other toilet-trained child, Elaine put her in regular underpants and took her to the mall for an afternoon of lunch and shopping. It was in a rather upscale store that the puddle of urine around Maggie's feet reminded Elaine that they had not visited the ladies' room after lunch. Poor Maggie cried with embarrassment and shame as three unsympathetic salesladies scurried around looking for paper towels to give Elaine for the cleanup.

In the best-case scenario, your child is never too far from his potty seat during toilet training. In the real world, however, life goes on even during toilet training and you may find yourself far from home and toilet with your child tugging at your sleeve. In this case, the best hope for stress-free training is in preparation.

Be Prepared

Remember that your child has only primitive control over urinary muscles. He can't "wait" for very long. If you insist that he "hold it" until you find a toilet, you're likely to be cleaning up an accident. Before going on a trip, you can help your child learn to extend the time between the call to go and the time of muscle release. When he says he has to go to the potty at home, delay a few minutes. Let him practice holding tight his sphincter muscle. This will also give you a good idea of how long he can wait.

Before beginning your trip, prepare your child by talking about the bathroom arrangements. Describe what she can expect the bathrooms to look like in planes, trains, or buses. Talk about going on grownup toilets in restaurant bathrooms. If you're going camping, discuss how toileting will be handled.

When traveling, there may be no bathroom for many miles of highway; the bathrooms in trains, buses, or airplanes may have long lines waiting to get in and may be dirty once you get there. So plan ahead:

- Institute a household policy that everyone go to the bathroom immediately before leaving the house.
- When you know a restroom won't be available, limit your child's intake of drinks.
- Expect accidents. Some children regress in their training while away from home. Unfamiliar toilets can make a child very insecure (some children refuse to use them). Even an unfamiliar flushing sound can frighten a child away from the toilet. Others feel disoriented in their schedule and that can cause regression.
- Bring a complete change of clothing. Having an accident is difficult enough without having to sit in wet clothing for the rest of the trip, so bring underwear, pants, and socks. Have the child wear a pair of rubber or plastic pants over his regular training

pants. Some are terry lined to be even more absorbent.

- Bring a portable potty with you. Models that fold or are inflatable are available, with disposable liners. If you are teaching your child to use the toilet instead of a potty chair, you might want to travel with a portable adapter to place on top of a toilet seat for your child. (See Appendix A for product information.)
- Bring a lidded potty with you in the car. If your child can't wait until you reach a restroom, you can pull over to the side of the road and use the potty there. The lid prevents spills and keeps odors confined as much as possible. (Don't let your child use the potty while the car is in motion. It's unsafe for a young child to be unstrapped and outside the carseat while the car is moving.)
- Don't forget to bring baby wipes. They're great for bottom-wiping and for washing hands when there's no sink.
- Many public restrooms are dirty and unsanitary. Bring disinfectant sprays with you to sanitize the toilet seats. Always cover the toilet seat if your child is sitting down. You can buy toilet-seat covers for this purpose or use toilet paper.

On the Road

Once you're on the road, toileting problems are best solved with creative solutions and a sense of humor. This is, afterall, a normal, developmental stage that children all over the world go through. Training on the road, just adds a degree of challenge. Keep these tips in mind:

- Your child is bound to ask to go to the bathroom at inconvenient times, in shops, supermarkets, and banks with no public restrooms. Don't be shy about asking to use the staff facilities; it's rare that they'd prefer a puddle on the floor.
- Disposable training pants are a good way to keep the training going while preparing for the unavoidable accidents that can happen while traveling. If your child won't give up her new underwear for

disposables, you might bring along a diaper for emergencies only . Explain to your child that the diaper will be used only when no potty is available and she will need to wear it for just a few minutes.

- Expect that your child may need to go to the bathroom more often than usual. Children's urinary systems are still immature and they may react to the excitement of travel by needing to go to the bathroom. Try to be accommodating even when it's inconvenient. Be ready to stop in at public restrooms more often than you're used to.

- Don't rule out taking your child to the head of a line waiting for the restroom. Explain that your child can't wait a second longer; most people will gladly let you cut into line.

PART IV

Special Children

Chapter Fifteen

Training the Mentally Challenged Child

Certainly, children who are mentally challenged can be toilet trained, but they may train later and often the training takes longer than it does for other children. That's why these children need an extra dose of patience, guidance, and understanding from you.

It's true, of course, that children with mental disabilities vary greatly in their capabilities and physical health. The toilet-training program in this chapter is appropriate for children who are not institutionalized and who meet these criteria:

1. ____ Over age 2½
2. ____ Can walk by themselves
3. ____ Have motor control (can dress and undress with minimal assistance)
4. ____ Have at least partial sight
5. ____ Respond to simple commands

Unless your child has a medical problem that prohibits the possibility of independent toilet training, children who meet the above standards can be toilet trained. As always, it's a good idea to give your child's physician a call before you begin, to make sure there are no medical conditions or problems that would make training inadvisable at this time.

Daytime Control

Step One: Prepare Yourself

Before you begin toilet training your child, take some time to prepare yourself and your child's environment.

Get Some Background

It's important at this point that you read Chapter Two "Ready, Set, Go." This chapter helps you set the stage in your house and in your heart for your venture into toilet training. Here you are asked to evaluate your attitude, expectations, bathroom vocabulary, and view of rewards and punishments. All of these things are key components of successful training. Although most of the information applies to all children, remember to adjust some of the recommendations and age suggestions to the individual needs of your child. How long training takes, for example, will depend on your child's level of disability and his awareness of his body and sensations. The usual toilet-training age for children with mild to moderate mental disabilities is three to five years.

Talk It Over

Read Chapter 13, "Training with a Care-giver" if your child spends time each day in school or with someone other than yourself. The willingness of all those involved in your child's daily care to follow the same procedures is absolutely vital to success. Your child needs consistency in toileting routines and expectations; any deviation will delay his progress. Plan to call the care-givers every day (at least in the beginning) so that you can monitor progress and deal with any problems.

Examine Your Own Motives

Of course, it will be nice for *you* when your child is out of diapers, but freedom from dirty diapers shouldn't be the strongest motive behind your desire to toilet train your child at this time. The goal of toilet training is not merely to keep the child clean of excrement, but to elevate the child to the highest level of functioning possible by teaching self-initiated toileting. You want to train your child so that ultimately he is motivated to toilet himself on his own initiative without prompting of any sort. You are actually using toilet training to help your child learn to function independently and with social awareness.

Normal individuals toilet themselves to avoid the embarrassment of having an accident. Your child, too, can learn to keep his pants clean and dry by frequently toileting himself and thereby reducing the number of accidents he will have. This is your goal.

Map Out the Right Time

The amount of time needed to toilet train your child depends on a number of factors and varies from one child to the next. You can improve your chances of quick progress by choosing a training period that is relatively free of distractions and interruptions. Choose a time that is not hectic with holiday preparations, a time that is routine rather than exceptional (as it is during vacation time), a time that offers you the opportunity to give your child a bit more undivided attention than usual. If you choose your time well, and follow the training program with strict consistency, you can expect to see clearly evident initial progress within the first week or two of training.

Get Your Equipment Ready

There are certain "tools of the trade" you will need during your toilet-training process. you should have all these on hand before you begin.

- **Potty Chair.** Potty chairs and toilet seat adaptors are discussed in detail in Chapter Two. There are many styles to choose from, so you might want to ask your child's doctor if he or she recommends a certain kind. It's most important that your child feel comfortable and secure when sitting on the "pot."
- **Rewards.** This program of toilet training relies on prompt (within a few seconds) use of rewards for proper toileting. In addition to praise, you will need some kind of material reward such as a cookie, candy, stickers, or a small toy to motivate your

child to repeat the correct toileting act. Be sure to read the section "Rewards" in Chapter Three on page 73; this will give you some good ideas on what to stock up on.

- **Extra Clothing.** In the beginning, your child will have accidents during the training process. Be sure to have lots of clean, dry clothes available. It's important that soiled clothes be changed immediately so your child (and you) will know when dry clothes are staying dry and when they become wet again. The clothes your child wears during this time should be easy to get on and off. Avoid pants with buttons and zippers; use pants with an elastic waist. Girls sometimes find it easier and more comfortable to wear short dresses during training.

Your child will also need a full supply of underpants or training pants during this time. Once the training period has begun, do not let your child wear a diaper (even the new pull-up "training" diapers) during daytime training hours. The training relies on your child's ability to distinguish dry pants from wet pants; diapers confuse the matter.

Taking pants down and up again is a part of the toilet-training process. This is a skill that can be practiced in the weeks before training begins. Knowing how to do this will give your child one less thing to think about during the toilet-training period.

- **Pants Alarm.** You can purchase a special training device called a pants alarm. (See Appendix A for purchasing information.) There are several different types on the market today; each sounds an alarm when urine moistens the child's underwear. The purpose of this pants alarm is to alert your child (and you) at the moment urine is released. This helps your child recognize the sensation and it allows you to immediately respond with the procedure for accidents that is described later in this chapter. The use of this device may help your child progress more rapidly through his toilet training, but it is not an essential part of the training procedure and it should never be used in place of your personal prompting and attention. It is most appropriate in situations in which the child spends time without close supervision from care-giving adults and accidents cannot be immediately detected.

Equipment Checklist:

1. ____ Potty chair or toilet seat adaptor
2. ____ Rewards
3. ____ Extra clothing and underpants
4. ____ Pants alarm (optional)

Observation Period

By now, your child has probably developed a fairly regular pattern of elimination. If you know approximately when your child is going to have a bowel movement, you can guide him to the toilet at that time to improve his chances of toileting success. During the week *before* you intend to begin toilet training, use the "Patterns of Elimination" chart, which follows on page 202 to keep a record of his bowel movements (which are easiest to track). (A sample chart is on page 60). You can also observe the frequency of urination if you stay attentive after your child has had liquid to drink. After your child has had a drink, check his diaper every few minutes to find out how long it takes for him to urinate; then record it on the chart.

If your chart shows that your child is not having a bowel movement every day or two, his constipation should be addressed before you begin training. One of the keys to helping children regulate their bowel movements is to help ensure stool consistency that is fairly firm without being too hard. Constipation is a common problem in children with multiple disabilities because they are often inactive and they may eat inadequate amounts of fiber and drink too few fluids. Preventing constipation through a sensible and individualized bowel-management program is the best approach to this problem. Be sure to read "Constipation Control" on page 149 if your child's "Pattern of Elimination" chart shows that he is not having a bowel movement every day or two. Also watch to see if his stools are large, hard, and difficult to pass.

PATTERNS OF ELIMINATION

Timmy							
Date:	6/5	6/6	6/7	6/8			
Times:							
7:00 A.M.							
8:00		BM					
9:00	BM		BM	BM			
10:00							
11:00							
12:00 P.M.							
1:00							
2:00							
Continue throughout the day							

Are You Ready?

1. ____ Contact your child's doctor
2. ____ Contact your child's care-takers to explain the details of this training program and gain their cooperation
3. ____ Evaluate child's undressing and dressing abilities and provide opportunities to practice these skills before training
4. ____ Obtain items on equipment list
5. ____ Complete the Patterns of Elimination chart

Step Two: Begin the Toilet-Training Program

The toilet-training procedures described below are based on many years of research by our nation's leading child psychologists and physicians. Although there are some minor variations from program to program, the process outlined in this chapter presents the basics of the standard protocol used in the toilet training of mentally challenged children. Field testing has found that the results are readily replicated provided the procedures are followed exactly.

There are 4 parts of this program:

1. Scheduled toileting
2. Rewarding success
3. Pants checks
4. Positive practice for accidents

1. Scheduled Toileting

Scheduled toileting assures that your child has frequent opportunities to use the toilet. This means that the entire process of toileting is completed at least once or twice *every* hour. The process includes:

- Walking to the toilet
- Lowering pants
- Sitting on the toilet
- Raising pants
- Washing hands

It's not necessary to schedule toileting at the exact same times every day. It's more helpful to schedule toilet visits at times when success is most likely: following meals and snacks, or after the child has had liquids to drink. (Some toileting programs for the mentally challenged advise giving the child more fluids than usual to prompt the need to urinate.)

The goal of this training is to teach your child independent toileting, not simply to teach the child to obey your directions. Therefore, don't *take* your child to the bathroom every half hour; instead, first ask, "Do you have to go potty?" Then encourage your child to say, "Potty," and guide him to the bathroom. Only if your child says, "No," should you physically, but gently, guide him to the bathroom anyway, with a cheerful, "Well, let's just try."

During the toileting process, give as little prompting and guidance as possible to help your child go through all the steps. At first, of course, you'll be more actively helping, but eventually you want your child to initiate the visits to the bathroom and to follow each of the steps without help. Let him pull down his own pants; let him get on the potty by himself; let him get off and pull up his pants himself. When he's able, let him practice wiping himself clean, and let him use a step stool (if necessary) to wash and dry his hands by himself.

Talk to your child about what you are doing every time he goes into the bathroom. Say to him, "It's time to go to the potty." Then encourage him to say it back to you, asking, "What time is it?" When you're ready to leave the bathroom, ask your child, "What did you just do?" If your child can't answer, supply the word, "potty," and ask the question again. Continue asking and supplying the answer throughout the day until your child can answer without any help from you.

When your child does initiate toileting by saying "potty," encourage him to go immediately. Don't worry that it's not on schedule. If he goes to the toilet and nothing happens, that's okay! The practice of walking to the toilet, lowering pants, sitting on the toilet, and raising pants is always a good exercise. Always praise these efforts; never scold for sounding a false alarm.

2. Rewarding Success

Your child's willingness and ability to achieve independent toileting habits can be encouraged with a liberal supply of rewards. Your praise and attention for successfully completing any of the toileting steps will encourage your child to want to do it again.

In addition to praise, you can increase cooperation with a stash of fun rewards. Chapter Three, pages 73–74, outlines a number of reward ideas that are often successful with children. Things like stickers, stars, candles, and cookies can be given to your child each time he completes any of the toileting steps. Be sure to put as much emphasis as possible on rewarding successful toileting because it is a very important part of the program.

As your child gets more accustomed to the toileting procedure, you may decide to give rewards only for self-initiated bathroom visits, and then later only for actually putting urine or bowel movements in the bowl. Eventually, rewards can be phased out completely.

3. Dry Pants Check

The dry pants check has two purposes: 1) to allow you and your child to detect accidents, and 2) to provide repeated opportunities for you to reward your child when the pants are found to be dry.

Between scheduled toiletings, periodically ask your child, "Are your pants dry?" Prompt your child to feel his crotch area and answer. When the answer is yes, reward your child with your praise or a small treat as explained above.

If your child spends much time away from a supervising adult, you may need to consider using a pants alarm that (by its silence) lets you know when the child is dry and deserves praise, and also signals when the child has had an accident.

When your child or the alarm notes an accident, move to the next step in the training program, called "Positive Practice for Accidents."

4. Positive Practice for Accidents

When you find that your child has wet or soiled his pants, the child should immediately be taken through these positive practice procedures:

1. Firmly admonish your child by holding his shoulders (to ensure attention) and saying, "No, you wet/dirtied your pants!"
2. Immediately and quickly guide your child to the toilet, using firm guidance.
3. Prompt your child to clean himself and change his pants (using guidance to make sure it is done quickly) and say, "You wet/dirtied your pants; now you have to practice."
4. Have the child proceed through the entire toileting sequence at least five times. Each sequence should begin as close as possible to the point where the accident occurred. The sequence proceeds like this: the child walks to the toilet, lowers his pants, briefly sits on the toilet (3–5 seconds), stands up, raises his pants, washes his hands, and then returns to the place where the accident occurred.

Following the practice, your child can return to what he was doing before the accident, and you should resume scheduled toileting.

Important points:

- Positive practice should be done immediately upon detection of an accident.
- Do not scold or punish accidents; use a matter-of-fact attitude.
- Do not let your child get out of positive practices by throwing a tantrum. With a firm attitude, guide your child through the steps despite his anger; this will teach your child that the practice is a necessary and inevitable consequence for accidents.

If positive practice is conducted immediately, consistently, and thoroughly, the child should quickly learn the routine and, before long, learn to use the toilet instead of his or her pants.

Hygiene

Proper hygiene habits should be practiced throughout the entire program, even though much reminding may be necessary in the beginning. Following each success, good hygiene can be practiced by guiding the child's hand to the toilet paper dispenser, removing a small amount, and then helping the child wipe the soiled body part. You should gradually reduce your involvement by using less and less guidance of the child's hands until he can wipe independently. In addition, following each success, the child should wash and dry his hands before leaving the bathroom.

Completing the Program

If this toilet-training program is faithfully carried out, you should see evidence of progress within about one week. Some children may progress more rapidly than others because the rate of progress will depend on many factors, including consistency, the number of opportunities for early success, and the amount of previous control displayed by the child. If any accidents go undetected or do not immediately result in positive practice, the program will be slowed down.

The entire training program should be continued without interruption until your child goes for at least three days without accidents in all settings. At this time, your child should be completing each step without physical guidance (although some assistance may be needed for thorough wiping and cleaning). When the child achieves this level, the pants alarm can be removed (if you were using one). Dry pants checks should be continued, as should the procedures for rewarding successes. If, during this period, an accident is not detected immediately, the child should be prompted to feel his or her wet pants when the accident is detected and should then proceed through the positive practice routine.

When your child goes another week without accidents, the dry pants checks and rewards can be reduced. It is recommended that the positive practice be kept in effect. However, as accidents become very infrequent and as the child continues to display independence, the reward procedure is not as vital as it was during the initial stages.

When your child completes an accident-free month, it is safe to say that toilet training is complete. After this period of solid success, it is rare to see a recurrence of chronic accidents that is not related to illness. (Although, as for all children, occasional accidents or regression can be expected.)

Nighttime Control

Once toilet training has begun, bed-wetting among all children is far more common than daytime accidents. Statistics show that at the age of six, about ten percent of normal children still wet their beds. This same delay in nighttime bladder control applies to mentally challenged children too, but to a greater extent. Without hands-on help, many of these children continue bed-wetting for many years after daytime control has been mastered.

The program for helping older children with bed-wetting described in Chapter 12 may work for your child also. Read through this chapter carefully and follow the program called "The Combined Approach" on page 173. This method has proven successful with some children who have mild mental disabilities.

If this program is not successful, or if you wish to begin with a more intensive program that offers a greater likelihood of success, you can try the program outlined in this chapter. It is adapted from a program first introduced years ago by Richard M. Foxx and Nathan H. Azrin, which offers a technique that can rather quickly help your child attain nighttime dryness.

Don't Rush into Nighttime Training

Training to eliminate bed-wetting should not be attempted until your child has first learned to toilet himself independently during the day. If your child is still having accidents during the day when he is mentally alert and attentive to his state, when his wetting is easily and quickly detected, and when toileting is not interfering with his sleep, then efforts to train him at night will be frustrating and generally unsuccessful. First train your child to be dry during the day. Then train him to be dry at night.

Be Optimistic

Many parents in your situation are so overwhelmed by their daytime schedules and responsibilities that they convince themselves that "my child will never be dry during the night." Night training is one more thing to add to their list of chores when the problem can more easily be handled with diapers.

Of course, you know that soon your child will grow up and be too old for diapers—and never have had the training he needs to stay dry at night. Although this program will persistently interrupt your sleep for a night or two, it's certainly worth a try. Following the instructions below, almost any child who has been daytime toilet trained can be taught to keep his bed dry at night. Exceptions to this statement apply to children with physical disorders that prevent bladder control and to the very young child (below age four) whose bladder and sphincter muscles may not be sufficiently developed to allow the retention of urine throughout an entire night. If you begin the program and encounter problems with your young child, first make sure he has no physical disorders that prohibit nighttime training. If there are no physical problems, try giving him more time to allow the bladder to develop.

Once you decide it's time to begin nighttime toilet training, the process is rather quick. The average bed-wetter can be trained in only one or two nights. After this intensive training, you can expect occasional regression, but unless your child experiences circumstances that discourage nighttime toileting (like a cold room temperature that discourages self-toileting, excessive fluid intake prior to bedtime, illness, or intestinal disorders) you can expect your child to attain complete independent nighttime toileting.

Get Ready

To prepare for nighttime training, you'll need a few supplies on hand before you begin:

- A urine alarm that is placed on the mattress before bedtime (See Appendix A for purchasing information)
- A variety of fluids that your child likes to drink
- Reward treats like candy or cookies
- A kitchen or pocket timer

An Overview

The nighttime toilet-training program for mentally challenged children follows these five steps:

1. Hourly training and rewards
2. Immediate detection of accidents
3. Disapproval of accidents
4. Nighttime cleanliness training and positive practice
5. Monitored maintenance

Step One: Hourly Training and Rewards

At bedtime, give your child an opportunity to go to the bathroom and require him to drink about two cups of fluids.

Then, every hour throughout the night, awaken your child and tell him to feel his dry bed. (Use a kitchen or pocket timer to wake yourself up.) Have your child go to the toilet and sit for at least five minutes. If he does not urinate, direct him back to his room and give him two cups of fluid before returning to his bed. If he does urinate, immediately praise him. After urination is completed, embrace him, prompt him to flush the toilet and wash his hands, and then give him treat rewards. Then direct him back to his room and give him two more cups of fluids. Repeat this procedure every hour during the night.

Step Two: Immediate Detection of Accidents

Most often, bed-wetting happens because the child is not awake enough to realize he is urinating and because you're not there to point out the act of wetting as quickly as you can during the day.

A urine alarm on the mattress overcomes these problems by producing a sound as soon as bed-wetting starts. This instantly alerts the bed-wetter (and you) that an accident has occurred. This is vitally important to the success of this program. The details of the urine alarm are described on page 173 in Chapter 12, and purchasing information is available in Appendix A and from your pharmacist.

If, in between your hourly awakenings, you hear the urine alarm, go to your child and follow Step Three procedures.

Step Three: Disapproval of Accidents

The purpose of Step Three is to teach your child that bed-wetting is not acceptable. When the urine alarm signals an accident, go to your child. Wake him if he's not awake already. Gently grasp his shoulders to make him look you in the eye, and with a look of disapproval say, "No, you wet your bed." Then turn off the urine alarm and send your child to the toilet to finish urinating. While your child is toileting, remove the urine alarm and wipe it clean. (Your child should never handle the alarm.)

Step Four: Nighttime Cleanliness Training and Positive Practice

Step Four will teach your child that he is responsible for cleaning the bed that he has wet and that he must practice correct toileting if he has an accident.

When your child returns, instruct him to change into dry clothing and put his wet pajamas in the appropriate place (use as little guidance as possible). Then it's time to take care of the bed and bed linens. Instruct your child to remove the soiled linen and bring it to the appropriate place. Then tell him to get clean linens and remake his bed (after you reconnect the urine alarm and put on the bottom sheet). Again, use as little manual guidance as possible; you want your child to feel responsible for this activity. Talk to your child in neutral tones and remain calm.

After your child has made his bed let him lie down on his bed for about two minutes (this duplicates the normal sleeping situation in which he is expected to rouse himself from a relaxed state). At the end of the two minutes, rouse your child and escort him to the toilet. Require him to lower his pants and sit on the toilet for about 30 seconds. At the end of the 30 seconds, escort him back to his bed.

Repeat these steps about ten times (or until 45 minutes have passed since the urine alarm sounded). Do not reward your child if he urinates during this practice period. Otherwise, he may deliberately wet his bed hoping to get the reward.

As time consuming as this process is, most children learn to stay dry within the first night of training; almost none require more than three nights.

Step Five: Monitored Maintenance

Monitored maintenance is begun on the night immediately following training. In this stage, stop giving your child fluids and stop the hourly awakenings, but leave the urine alarm on the bed. If your child has an accident, repeat Step Four: Nighttime Cleanliness and Positive Training. This will reinforce the message that he is still responsible for his actions.

When your child does not wet his bed for seven consecutive nights, take the urine alarm off the bed and check the sheets for dryness each morning. If dry, praise and reward your child. If wet, require him to remake the bed with clean linens.

If your child has two accidents during any seven-day period, put the urine alarm back on his bed and reinstitute the Cleanliness Training and Positive Practice every time the alarm sounds. Do this until he does not wet his bed for seven consecutive nights.

This method of nighttime training does ask a lot of you—your time, your commitment, and your sleep. But so has every other developmental milestone your child has accomplished. With this relatively quick process, your child will gain a sense of responsibility and independence so important to healthy growth. You will also give him a reason to feel proud of himself every morning for the rest of his life.

Chapter Sixteen

Training the Physically Challenged Child

This chapter addresses the needs of children who are physically challenged and may use a wheelchair, leg braces, or walkers. The information is appropriate for children who have use of their arms and hands, have voluntary control over their sphincter muscles, and with training are physically capable of independent toileting. The following is a general guide to help you prepare for and understand the special needs of these children.

Generally, physically challenged children over the age of three who have normal cognitive abilities can train with the toilet-training philosophies and methods described in Chapters One, Two, and Three. Obviously, there may be more initial parental involvement in taking off the pants and wiping afterwards, but like all parents, you should make a conscious effort to gradually reduce the amount of help you offer, with the goal of eventually transferring the entire toileting process over to your child.

Many children with physical disabilities also have cognitive impairments and will need a toilet-training program that combines the guidelines in this chapter with the ones in Chapter Fifteen.

In any case, you will need to work closely during this venture with your child's doctors and therapists. They know your child's individual abilities and needs and are a valuable resource of information and support.

A Lot to Learn

Physically challenged children have more to learn during toilet training than others. Not only are they learning to be responsible for controlling when and where they go to the bathroom, they also must eventually learn to undress, redress, and transfer themselves from their chair or appliance to the toilet.

The order of events depends on your preference. You may choose to practice toilet training first by carrying your young child to and from the toilet or potty seat. Once the child is completely toilet trained, then you can introduce the skills of dressing and transferring from the wheelchair or appliance. Or, you may prefer to teach toilet training, dressing, and transfers at the same time. Either way, the ultimate goal is independent toileting in which your child will take himself to the toilet, remove his pants, transfer to the toilet or potty, wipe himself afterward, redress, and then wash his hands. These are a lot of steps for a physically challenged child to master, but with your help he can do it and gain an immeasurable boost in self-esteem.

Adaptations

Special Potty Seats

Regular potty seats and toilets may not be appropriate for your child's special needs. Many commercial potty seats are rather flimsy and your toilet seat may not be secure enough for the physical needs of your child. You can buy specially adapted seats—some stand alone; others attach to your toilet—that will make the whole process of toilet training much easier for your child. These seats provide back and side support for a child who does not have adequate sitting balance. Many will position the child with the body leaning forward, hips flexed (more than 90 degrees), and feet supported. This position is best for children who have low tone (which makes it difficult for the child to increase abdominal pressure for toileting). It's especially important for children with increased extensor tone (as common with cerebral palsy), because this flex position breaks up the extensor pattern (the tendency to extend the bodies to an open position) and will make sitting on the potty safe. Some models keep the child's arms and shoulders forward while providing space for toys or books. This table should automatically lock into place and provide a secure support. These adaptive seats give children the sense of security they need to relax for potty training. See Appendix A for purchasing information.

Once you decide that it's time for your child to begin toileting without being completely dependent on you, you'll need to talk to your child's occupational therapist to find out how your bathroom may need to be adapted for this move. You will need to install grab bars on the walls to help your child transfer and stand if he's able. If your child is in a wheelchair, the bathroom doorway will have to be widened and the room made wheelchair accessible.

Dry-Run Practice

Sensory Awareness

Sometimes children with physical disabilities have decreased body awareness that limits their ability to tell when they are wet or dry. Before your begin toilet training, work a bit with your child to help him clearly distinguish between wet and dry. While bathing take two washcloths; submerge one in water and keep the other dry. Have your child tell you which one is wet and which one is dry. Pour water on one of his hands (when they are dry) and ask him again, which one is dry and which one is wet. When washing clothes, take one pair of wet pants and one pair of dry and ask your child to point to the dry pair. These little exercises will help children better understand what is happening when they're out of diapers and have an accident. You can point to the wet pants and ask, "Are your pants dry or wet?" This information will help your child set the personal goal of staying dry by going to the toilet or potty.

Feeling Secure

It's really important that your child feel secure while sitting on the toilet or potty before you begin to actually toilet train. Your child may be afraid of falling, and this fear alone causes many to resist toilet training completely. While fully clothed, let your child sit on the toilet seat or potty chair. Let him practice sitting on the seat until you're sure he feels confident. Without this sense of physical safety, you can lose this battle before you even get going.

Clothing

Independent toileting requires that a person can take down pants and underwear and then pull them back up again. This task will be easier for your child if he wears very loose clothing. It takes a physically challenged child much longer to pull down pants and if this process is too difficult, you'll have accidents while your child is positioned right in front of the toilet or potty. Use easy pull-off pants with no buttons or zippers. Use loose-fitting underpants that come off quickly.

Then, before your child arrives at the toilet with a full bladder, practice undressing and redressing in the bathroom. Again, your occupational therapist can explain how, depending on your child's capabilities, this is best accomplished. But whatever the method, calm, unhurried practice is the best teacher.

Transfers

Before you begin independent training, set aside time to help your child learn how to transfer from his chair or appliance to the toilet or potty. Your therapist will show you exactly how to do this safely and with the greatest ease possible. This skill should first be practiced fully clothed without mention of toileting until your child feels secure and confident. Gradually offer less and less assistance, until your child is able to do it himself.

Successful Toileting

Prompting

Even after your child has mastered toilet training, continue to prompt him every few hours with a simple reminder like, "Do you have to go to the bathroom now?" When children are busy and involved in their activities, they all wait until the last second to go to the bathroom. For a child with physical disabilities, this is usually disastrous because it takes so long to transfer out of the wheelchair, walker, or braces and get the pants down. They need to leave themselves lots of time and your prompting and reminding will help them do that.

Hygiene

Some children with physical handicaps have a difficult time wiping themselves after toileting, but most children can learn with a few adaptations and persistence. Although many children normally reach around to wipe themselves from the back, this movement may be difficult for your child. You may have to teach him to wipe from the front, going in between the legs. Be especially careful to explain to little girls why they must wipe from the front to the back, so they don't bring the germs from bowel movements into the vaginal area, where they can cause infection.

If cleaning remains a problem or your child is developmentally unable to properly wipe after toileting, ask your therapist about the possibility of installing a bidet-type device into the toilet that will help your child clean himself. Toileting is a lifelong activity, so it is usually worth the expense.

Washing hands is also a part of toileting. If your child is able to reach the sink, be sure to remind him to wash after every trip to the toilet or potty. If he cannot reach the sink, you might find it easiest to keep a container of antiseptic wipes near the toilet for convenient use. Because personal hygiene is a lifelong need, you might also consider installing an adaptive sink for the ease and convenience of your child.

Cooperation with Care-givers and Teachers

If your child spends time each day with another family member or a sitter, or if he is in school, you'll need to talk to these people about your plans for toilet training. A positive outcome depends on the cooperation of all the people who care for your child.

If your child is in a school for special-needs children, his teacher can be a great help in guiding you through this experience. Be sure to sit down and talk about the methods and adaptive equipment the school uses; it will help your child if you use the same at home. Share information your doctor or therapist has given you about your child's specific toilet-training needs. Plan to keep in touch with the teacher to compare notes and keep up on your child's progress at school. (Sometimes children will toilet independently at school but not at home, where they feel comfortable remaining dependent on their parents.)

If your child spends time with a sitter, you're in charge of explaining the toilet-training method you want to use. Make sure his care-givers know every detail of the toileting process you are using when your child is at home with you. If everybody agrees to reinforce one another, your child will be the big winner in the end. Be sure to read all the details of toilet training with a care-giver in Chapter Thirteen.

Independence

You may find that your child resists independent toilet training because he has learned to be dependent on you to take care of all his physical needs. He may not even want to cue into what happens physically when he urinates or has a bowel movement. His bodily functions have always been taken care of by somebody else. This is the perfect time to introduce personal responsibility. Now is the time to let your child know that he too has to help take care of himself.

As your child gets older, care-givers and teachers will be less willing to take on the job of toileting. They certainly don't want to be changing diapers on an eight-year-old who is capable of independent toileting. And they'll soon tire of bringing your child to the bathroom, taking off his pants, getting him on the toilet, and wiping him afterward.

Your child may start toilet training later than your neighbor's kids, and he may take longer to become fully independent, but with your help and persistence in teaching him to do it for himself, eventually he will be proud to have one more area in which he can be independent.

A Word After

As stated in the first chapter, my goal in writing this book has been to gather together all the available information on toilet training, sort out the research on the most effective methods, and present them in a simple and easy-to-understand manner. I'm not recommending one method over another. All of them work for different children, with different needs, under different circumstances. It's now your job to choose the one that is most appropriate for you and your child. To do this, you have to consider your child's individual needs, abilities, physical development, and level of maturity, as well as your own needs, temperament, and work schedule.

Whichever method you choose, some aspects of toilet training remain constant. All toilet training is best accomplished if you follow these guidelines:

- Take on the role of a teacher and encourage your child and give him specific directions.
- Avoid the extremes of being too strict or too lax.
- Maintain a warm and loving attitude.
- Stay calm and confident.
- Give more positive feedback than negative.
- Don't over- or underestimate your child.
- Set realistic expectations.
- Expect regression and don't overreact when it happens.

- Show confidence in your child's abilities by expressing a positive expectation of success.
- Pick out one method of toilet training that is best suited for you and your child—not for your friends and relatives.

APPENDIX A

TOILET-TRAINING PRODUCTS

Toilet Trainers

Freestanding Potty Seats

- *Toilette Plus Trainer:* Three-part system featuring stable base with lift-up lid and removable receptacle. Seat detaches for use on an adult toilet; base becomes a step stool. Cosco, at mass-merchandise and juvenile specialty stores.
- *Fisher-Price Potty:* Three-stage potty has no lid, but includes a splash guard and training booklet. For a store near you, call 1–800–432–KIDS
- *Gerry Potty Seat:* Front-access bowl and tilt-down deflector ensure easy cleanups; detachable seat snaps onto adult toilet. Gerry Baby Products. For a store near you, call 1–800–525–2472.
- *Two-Stage Trainer.* This potty seat sits low to the ground and in stage 2 fits over the toilet seat and offers a helpful non-slip step up. The Right Start Catalog, 1–800–LITTLE–1.

Travel Models

- *My Potty!:* Portable plastic ring, with fold-up legs that serves as a base for disposable plastic pouches.

Binky-Griptight, Inc. To order, or for a store near you, call 1–800–526–6320.

- *Travel Potty:* Wide plastic cup with snap-on lid for those long stretches between rest stations. Playskool Baby. For a store near you, call 1–800–PLAYSKL.
- *Cushie Tushie:* This thick and cushy seat makes a regular potty seat smaller so that it's the size of a two-year-old's tushie. Fits securely into most standard and elongated seats. The Right Start Catalog, 1–800–LITTLE–1.
- *Folding Potty Seat:* Good for home and travel, this plastic attachment turns any toilet seat into a sanitary potty seat, then folds and fits into a purse-size bag. Children on the Go. The Right Start Catalog, 1–800–LITTLE–1.

Large-Size Diapers

- *Pampers:* Large size available in Regular or Super Absorbency. For children weighing 19 to 35 pounds.
- *Huggies:* Toddler-size disposables fit children 23 pounds and up.

Training Pants

- *Huggies Pull-Ups Training Pants:* Disposable training pants with an elastic waist that look like "big-kid" briefs but provide the absorption and protection of a disposable diaper. Kimberly-Clark. At grocery and department stores.
- *Gerber Terry Training Pants:* Made of 100 percent cotton terry cloth. These pants have double-thick crotch, elastic leg and waistbands. Machine washable. Available from Gerber Products Co. at mass-merchandise stores.
- *Curity Training Pants:* Pants have extra-absorbency

center panel. Made with varying degrees of absorbency from the super soaker, featuring exclusive fiber sponge insert, to the triple-layer terry pants designed for the child's first underwear when occasional accidents could occur. Available from Soft Care Apparel, Inc. at mass-merchandise stores.

Urine Alarms

Your pediatrician may be able to direct you to a source for these alarms. They are also available through JC Penny catalogs. Many local pharmacies also carry these items.

Adaptive Equipment for Special-Needs Children

- *Kaye Products:* For a catalog call 1–919–732–6444 or fax 1–800–685–5293.
- *Rifton Products:* For a catalog call 1–800–374–3866.
- *Smith and Nephew Rolyan:* For a catalog call 1–800–558–8633.
- *Sammons Preston:* For a Catalog call 1–800–323–5547.

APPENDIX B

ADDITIONAL READING AND VIDEOS

For Parents

Toilet Training in Less Than a Day
Nathan H. Azrin, Ph.d. and Richard M. Foxx, Ph.s.
Simon & Schuster, 1974

Tricle Treat: Diaperless Toilet Training
Laurie Boucke. White-Boucke, 1991.

The Parents Book of Toilet Teaching
Joanna Cole. Ballantine Books, 1986.

Practical Parenting: Toilet Training
Vicki Lansky. Bantam Books, 1984.

Positive Potty Training
September Morn. Pawprince Press, 1995.

Potty Training Your Baby.
Katie Van Pelt. Avery Publishing Group, 1988.

For Children

I Lift the Lid
Pam Adams. Child's Play, 1995.

Annie's Potty
Judith Caseley. Greenwillow Books, 1990.

Potty Time
Anne Civardi. Simon & Schuster, 1993.

The King Sat on the Throne
Annie Kubler. Child's Play, 1995.

Uh Oh! Gotta Go!
Bob Mc Grath. Barron's Educational Series, 1996.

On Your Potty
Virginia Miller. Greenwillow Books, 1991.

I Have to Go
Anna Ross. Random House, 1990.

The Potty Chronicles
Annie Reiner. Magination Press, 1991.

Video

It's Potty Time
Developed by the Duke University Medical Center, this videotape demystifies toilet training with child actors and sing-alongs. Learning Through Entertainment, Inc, 1–800–445–5142.

Once Upon A Potty For Him
Once Upon a Potty for Her
These videos are the animated versions of the book of the same name by Alona Frankel. They feature a sing-along Potty Song; at the end of the tape a pediatrician answers questions. Baron's Home Video, 1–800–645–3476.

Training Toys

Piddlers
Cute little green and blue fish make colorful targets that encourage little boys to use the toilet and keep the bathroom cleaner. Fish float in the toilet bowl and then dis-

solve on a "direct hit." Non-toxic and eco-friendly. $6.95 for 10-pack from Right Start Catalog, 1–800–LITTLE–1.

Dolls that wet and are ready for toilet training include:

Baby Alive, from Kenner.

Betsy Wetsy, Tiny Tears, and *Magic Potty Baby,* from Tyco Toys.

Cabbage Patch Kids' Potty Seat, for their dolls from Hasbro.

Notes

Chapter One

1. Huschka, M. The Child's Response to Coercive Bowel Training. *Psychosomatic Medicine,* 1942, *4,* 301–308.
2. Sears, R. R., E. E. Maccoby, and H. Levin. *Patterns of Childrearing.* Stanford, CA: Stanford University Press, 1957.
3. Azrin, N. H. and R. M. Foxx. *Toilet Training in Less Than a Day.* New York: Simon & Schuster, 1974.
4. Hindley, C. B., A. M. Fillozat, G. Klackenberg, D. Nicolet-Meister, and E. A. Sand. Some differences in infant feeding and elimination training in five European longitudinal samples. *Journal of Child Psychology and Psychiatry,* 1965, *6,* 179–201.
5. deVries, M. W. and M. R. Cultural relativity of toilet training readiness. A perspective from East Africa. *Pediatrics,* 1977, *60,* 170–177.
6. Cohen, T. B. Observations on school children in the People's Republic of China. *Journal of Child Psychiatry,* 1977, *16,* 165–173.

Chapter Two

1. Sears, R. R., E. E. Maccoby, and H. Levin. *Patterns of Childrearing.* Stanford, CA: Stanford University Press, 1957.
2. Stein, A. and M. Susser. Social factors in the development of sphincter control. *Developmental Medicine and Child Neurology,* 1967, *9,* 692–706.
3. Fraiberg, S. H. *The Magic Years.* New York: Scribner, 1959.
4. Ilg, F. L. and L. Ames. *Child Behavior.* New York: Harper & Row, 1955.
5. Ilg, F. L., L. B. Ames, and S. Babe. *Child Behavior* (revised edition). New York: Harper & Row, 1981.

Chapter Three

1. Graubard, P. S. *Positive Parenthood.* New York: New American Library, 1978.

Chapter Four

1. Huschka, M. The child's response to coercive bowel training. *Psychosomatic Medicine,* 1942, *4,* 301–308.
2. deVries, M. W. and M. R. Cultural relativity of toilet training readiness. A perspective from East Africa. *Pediatrics,* 1977, *60,* 170–177.
3. Cohen, T. B. Observations on school children in the People's Republic of China, *Journal of Child Psychiatry,* 1977, *16,* 165–173.
4. Ball, T. S. Toilet training an infant mongoloid at the breast. *California Mental Health Research Digest,* 1971, *9,* 80–85.
5. Smeets, P. M., G. E. Lancioni, T. S. Ball, and D. S. Oliva. Shaping self-initiated toileting in infants. *Journal of Applied Behavior Analysis,* 1985, *18,* 303–308.

6. *Ibid.,* pp. 306–307.
7. Sears, R. R., E. E. Maccoby, and H. Levin. *Patterns of Childrearing.* Stanford, CA: Stanford University Press, 1957.

Chapter Five

1. Azrin, N. H. and R. M. Foxx. *Toilet Training in Less Than a Day.* New York: Simon & Schuster, 1974.

Chapter Ten

1. Wright, L. Handling the encopretic child. *Professional Psychology,* 1973, *4,* 137–144.
2. Gabel, S. (ed.). *Behavioral Problems in Childhood.* New York: Grune & Stratton, 1981.

Chapter Eleven

1. Richmond, G. Shaping bladder and bowel continence in developmentally retarded preschool children. *Journal of Autism and Developmental Disorders,* 1983, *13,* 197–204.

Chapter Twelve

1. Glicklich, L. B. An historical account of enuresis. *Pediatrics,* 1951, *8,* 859.

Chapter Fifteen

1. Foxx, R. M. and N. H. Azrin. *Toilet Training the Retarded.* Champaign, IL: Research Press, 1973.

Index

231

Ⓢ SIGNET

GUIDES FOR A HEALTHIER YOU

☐ **HARRIET ROTH'S FAT COUNTER** Eating right has never been easier with complete information on: fat percentages, fat grams, calories, cholesterol, and brand name comparisons.
(1//991—$2.99)

☐ **HARRIET ROTH'S GUIDE TO LOW CHOLESTEROL DINING OUT by Harriet Roth.** Now that Americans are eating out and traveling more than ever before, maintaining a low-cholesterol, low-fat diet on restaurant meals may seem almost impossible. But with this invaluable guide, you'll never again have to deny yourself the pleasures of fine dining. (169018—$2.99)

☐ **CHOLESTEROL Your Guide For A Healthy Heart by the Editors of *Consumer Guide*®.** Here is your map through the maze of cholesterol controversies, treatments, and "miracle cures." From the Editors of *Consumer Guide*®, with assistance from the National Institutes of Health, this up-to-date, authoritative guide can turn you into a heart-smart consumer. (822684—$7.99)

*Prices slightly higher in Canada
